Japan's Quest for Stability in Southeast Asia

More than any other region in the world, Asia has witnessed tremendous change in the post-war era. A continent once engulfed by independence and revolution, and later by the Cold War and civil war, has now been transformed into the world's most economically dynamic region. What caused this change in Asia? The key to answering this question lies in the post-war history of maritime Asia and, in particular, the path taken by the maritime nation of Japan.

Analyzing the importance of Japan's relationship with Southeast Asia, this book aims to illustrate the hidden trail left by Japan during the period of upheaval that has shaped Asia today—an era marked by the American Cold War strategy, the dissolution of the British Empire in Asia, and the rise of China. It provides a comprehensive account of post-war maritime Asia, making use of internationally sourced primary materials as well as declassified Japanese government papers. As such, *Japan's Quest for Stability in Southeast Asia* will be useful to students and scholars of Japanese Politics, Asian Politics and Asian History.

Taizo Miyagi is Professor in the Faculty of Global Studies at Sophia University, Japan. His recent publications include *Gendai Nihon gaiko-shi* (History of Contemporary Japanese Diplomacy, 2016).

Routledge Contemporary Japan Series

For a full list of titles in this series, please visit www.routledge.com.

Japan's Quest for Stability in Southeast Asia

Navigating the Turning Points in Postwar Asia

Taizo Miyagi

Translated by Hanabusa Midori

LONDON AND NEW YORK

JAPAN LIBRARY

First published 2018
by Routledge
2 Park Square, Milton Park, Abingdon, Oxon OX14 4RN

and by Routledge
711 Third Avenue, New York, NY 10017

Routledge is an imprint of the Taylor & Francis Group, an informa business

British Library Cataloguing-in-Publication Data
A catalogue record for this book is available from the British Library

Library of Congress Cataloging-in-Publication Data
A catalog record for this book has been requested

ISBN: 978-1-138-10372-6 (hbk)
ISBN: 978-1-315-10257-3 (ebk)

Typeset in Times New Roman
by codeMantra

Throughout the book, Japanese names are rendered in the Western order, given name followed by family name, except for the name of the translator.

Contents

Illustrations

Figures

Map

Foreword to the English edition

This book was written with the purpose of bridging several gaps in the history of international politics in Asia after World War II. One of them is the gap that exists between the perception of Asia in the early postwar years—from the end of the war to the mid-1960s—as a region enveloped by conflicts and wars of independence, wallowing in economic poverty and stagnation, and the perception of Asia since the 1970s, as a region characterized by development and economic growth. Once a political battlefield at the intersection of decolonization and the Cold War, Asia has since undergone rapid economic growth, dubbed the "East Asian miracle," to become the global center of growth today. No other region has experienced such dramatic change over the past seven decades since World War II. This postwar transformation can be understood as a process in which Asia shifted from decolonization to development.

The "decade of transition"—from 1965 to 1975—is crucial to any study of postwar Asia's transition from decolonization to development. This is the decade that began in 1965 with an aborted coup in President Sukarno's Indonesia known as the "September 30 Incident," a decade in which the rapprochement between the United States and China took place between 1971 and 1972 and lasted until the fall of Saigon in 1975 that ended the Vietnam War. On the eve of the September 30 Incident, Sukarno, who was supportive of the Communist Party of Indonesia—the largest Communist group in the non-Communist bloc—formed the "Beijing-Jakarta Axis" with China, which was pursuing a diplomacy of radicalism. The Axis threatened to engulf the region from the north to the south. Had Saigon fallen under these circumstances, it could have lent more credibility to the "domino theory," which predicted a successive spread of Communism from one country to another.

However, the September 30 Incident led to Sukarno's downfall. He was replaced by President Suharto, who sought to forge closer ties with Japan and the United States to build a system of economic development and moved towards the formation of the Association of South East Asian Nations (ASEAN). Having lost Sukarno as a partner in promoting radical diplomacy, China turned to the United States as a counterweight to the Soviet

Union. And by 1975, when the fall of Saigon brought an end to the Vietnam War, there were no longer any battles seeking independence from foreign rule being fought in Asia. It was the end of decolonization that set the stage for the subsequent tide of development and economic growth that spread to all corners of Asia. In this book, I have attempted to reveal the dynamics that governed the "decade of transition" and its historic background by focusing on Indonesia, which played a pivotal role in the development of postwar order in Asia.

This book also addresses another gap that existed between postwar Japan and the rest of Asia. Today, Japan enjoys intricate economic ties throughout Asia, to the extent that a virtual economic union is underway. Yet, Asia during the early postwar period was fraught with war and confusion—a region that felt so near, yet so far away for Japan, which had been the first to embark on a path to economic growth and had forged ahead towards becoming a developed nation. It was as though Japan had forgotten its past ambition of creating a Greater East Asia Co-Prosperity Sphere. As major events in international politics unfolded in postwar Asia, such as the Vietnam War and the US-China rapprochement, Japan played only a supportive role. However, once we reconstruct the axis that served as the basis for the historic transformation from decolonization to development that shaped the Asia of today, we are able to understand the significance of the role played by Japan. This book sheds light on the process through which postwar Japan re-entered Asia, and maritime Asia in particular, with a focus on Indonesia and the important role it eventually played during the "decade of transition."

I would be more than happy if the issues I raise and the framework of study I propose in this book are shared by a broader readership through the publication of this English edition.

Taizo Miyagi

About the author

Taizo Miyagi was born in Tokyo in 1968. He graduated from the Faculty of Law and Politics at Rikkyo University in 1992 and worked as a reporter at NIIK (Japan Broadcasting Corporation) until 1996. In 2001, he received a PhD from the Graduate School of Law and International Relations at Hitotsubashi University. His previous posts include Adjunct Instructor in the Faculty of Law and Politics at Rikkyo University, Assistant Professor in the Faculty of Law at Hokkaido University, Associate Professor at the National Graduate Institute for Policy Studies, and Associate Professor in the Department of International Relations at Sophia University. He is currently Professor in the Faculty of Global Studies at Sophia University. He has also written *Bandon Kaigi to Nihon no Ajia fukki* (The Bandung Conference and Japan's Return to Asia, Soshisha, 2001); *Sengo Ajia chitsujo no mosaku to Nihon* (Exploration of Postwar Asian Order and Japan, Sobunsha, 2004), which won the Suntory Prize for Social Sciences and Humanities; and *Gendai Nihon gaiko-shi* (History of Contemporary Japanese Diplomacy, Chuokoron-shinsha, 2016). He co-authored *Sengo Nihon no Ajia gaiko* (Japan's Postwar Diplomacy in Asia, Minerva Shobo, 2015), which won the Okita Memorial Prize for International Development Research in 2016. He has also received the Yasuhiro Nakasone Award for Excellence (2005) in recognition of his academic studies.

Prologue

If one were to write a history of international relations in Asia since World War II, how would Japan be positioned in such a narrative?

When the topic turns to Japan's past relationship with Asia, the so-called history issue—caused by different historical perspectives between Japan on the one hand and China and Korea on the other—might be the first thing that comes to mind for many. Given that the history issue consists of friction over interpretations and perceptions of incidents before and during World War II, however, it alone does not adequately explain the events that have unfolded over more than sixty years since the war.

In any attempt at identifying important issues in international politics in postwar Asia, the Korean War and the Vietnam War would no doubt figure prominently. Although economic ties among countries in the region have become so strong today that we even talk about forming an Asian community, postwar Asia has long been synonymous with turmoil and confusion more than anything else. And throughout this period, when Asia was characterized by war and turmoil, Japan appeared to devote all its energies to achieving economic growth for itself, showing little interest in international politics.

Japan regarded the Korean and Vietnam wars as somebody else's problem. Then, as the 1970s began, Japan was stunned by the sudden rapprochement between China and the United States, which had been the main adversaries of the Cold War in Asia. It was a cataclysmic event that took place behind Japan's back. Given such a track record of passivity, it seems almost futile to explore what Japan, a political weakling, means to Asia. Has Japan always been an insignificant player in the international politics of postwar Asia, a presence that is only relevant in the economic realm after all?

To answer the question about what Japan has been to postwar Asia, one must first consider what postwar Asia has been. Only after a blueprint of postwar Asia has been drawn can we assess with any accuracy the significance of Japan as its member.

The Cold War in Asia was an ideological conflict between Communists and non-Communists that manifested itself in the Korean and Vietnam wars. While it might have been a "cold war" for the leaders of the two conflicting camps—the United States, the Soviet Union, and China—a tremendous number of human lives were lost in the fierce "hot" wars on the Korean and Indochinese peninsulas, and tense diplomatic battles were fought to settle the conflicts. It should be obvious to anyone that the postwar history of Asia evolved around the Cold War.

> Darkness fell like fate on Saigon on April 29, 1975. By 6:30 p.m. a power cut had blacked out the city, but in a way, this was almost a blessing because it cloaked the shame of defeat. I stood on the terrace of the Hotel Caravelle under a fine drizzle, watching Saigon's last night…
>
> Below, a darkened and silent metropolis, known as both the Jewel of the Orient and the Whore City, awaited its conquerors. Its tall buildings were silhouetted against the flashes of rockets exploding over the horizon and the dull, orange glow of burning ammunition dumps at the Tan Son Nhut air base.[1]

On April 30, one day after the events described in the quote above, Saigon fell when the Communist forces rushed into the city. In this way, the Republic of Vietnam, or South Vietnam, perished from the earth. It was also the moment when the decades-long Vietnam War finally ended. Nayan Chanda writes, "I was dazed by the onrush of events, finding it hard to believe that the Vietnam War, a war that I had almost grown up with, had ended."[2] I suspect this sentiment was shared by many who belonged to the same generation as Chanda. The war in Vietnam, which had been fought incessantly since the end of World War II—first as the Indochinese War mainly against France and, subsequently, as the Vietnam War against the United States—had constantly remained at the center of the Asian political situation. Such as it was, when the war finally ended, it was with the swift, one-sided collapse of South Vietnam, an outcome that betrayed general expectations.

The end of the Vietnam War following the fall of Saigon could be viewed as the climax of the Cold War in Asia. Seen from this angle, we must question the impact and influence this climax has had on Asia in the decades since.

The United States, having predicted that the fall of South Vietnam would result in a fatal situation, not only for Vietnam and other Indochinese countries but for the entire Asian region as a whole, had continued to pour a tremendous number of troops as well as an enormous amount of funds into this remote area beyond the Pacific Ocean. The fear was that failure to suppress the Communist forces in Vietnam would trigger a domino-like phenomenon that would swallow its neighboring countries and, eventually, all of Asia in a sea of Communism. In actuality, however, the fall of Saigon signified the end of an era more than the beginning of a new situation long feared by the United States.

At the outset of his book *Imagined Communities: Reflections on the Origin and Spread of Nationalism*, a modern classic on nationalism, Benedict Anderson refers to Vietnam's invasion of Cambodia only a few years after the fall of Saigon and subsequent eruption of the Sino-Vietnamese War. Anderson states:

> These wars [i.e., the recent wars between Vietnam, Cambodia and China] are of world-historical importance because they are the first to occur between regimes whose independence and revolutionary credentials are undeniable, and because none of the belligerents has made more than the most perfunctory attempts to justify the bloodshed in terms of a recognizable *Marxist* theoretical perspective.[3]

Instead of a domino-like spread of Communism throughout Asia, what actually took place were wars between "brother states"—that is, Communist states that had won the fall of Saigon together as allies. Unlike the earlier Sino-Soviet confrontation, which had triggered a heated ideological dispute, contending parties in these wars (i.e., the Vietnamese invasion of Cambodia and the Sino-Vietnamese War) abandoned any attempts to justify them in terms of the Communist ideology, making them unexplainable by the Communist theory alone. In this sense, the fall of Saigon, which was undoubtedly a victory for the Eastern bloc, might have been, ironically, the beginning of the end of an era in which the Communist ideology was able to sustain its validity in Asia.

Thus, with the fall of Saigon, the Western camp realized that its fear of a domino-like spread of Communism would not come true, while the Eastern camp saw the fall of Saigon as marking the end of an era when the Communist ideology remained persuasive.

However, more profoundly, the fall of Saigon might have implied an end to an era when the pursuit of independence was the overwhelming goal that took precedence over any other causes in Asia.

In Japan, it has been customary to use August 1945 as the halfway point to divide the twentieth century into the period before and during the war, and the period after the war. People in Japan do not find this strange. For many other Asian countries, however, the march toward their independence— which was by far the greatest event in the twentieth century for them—began with the conclusion of World War II. In that sense, it was in the postwar period that "history" for them started moving dynamically.

It was the outpouring of people's energy for independence over time that fundamentally determined the direction of international politics in Asia after World War II. Because Communism succeeded in internalizing this energy, it was able to remain vigorous in Asia, promoting the Cold War in the region.

Needless to say, independence can be an ultimate goal only while it is yet to be attained. Once independence is achieved, it gives way to another, more substantial issue of nation-building. While before the fall of Saigon North Vietnam had been a shining star, enjoying a certain kind of respect in the world, it sank into a long period of stagnation and hardship once unification with the South was attained. This experience shows the stark contrast between the issues a nation must face before and after it attains independence.

What, then, fundamentally characterizes the history of postwar Asia? This was once a repository of ferocious political magma—one of revolution and nationalism—bursting out from the worldwide Cold War framework into regional hot wars. Once independence was attained, however, Asia accomplished outstanding economic growth to transform itself into a region with the world's greatest economic vitality. This became known as the East Asian miracle.

Thus, Asia has shown two faces in a span of half a century: the Asia that was once overflowing with political energy and the Asia that is now characterized by incomparable economic vigor. These two are so different that they almost seem to represent two different regions. And no other region in the world succeeded in accomplishing such a thorough transformation after World War II. It is this transformation that fundamentally characterizes the postwar development in Asia. Furthermore, the transformation was driven by historical forces that prompted the shift from decolonization to development, which coexisted in Asia along with the forces of the Cold War. These historical forces in postwar Asia are what this book aims to explore.

It has been customary in the past to think of international politics in postwar Asia as an Asian manifestation of the Cold War centered on the confrontation between China and the United States. As such, exploring Japan's position within that context may not seem to be much of a meaningful exercise. However, the Asian Cold War alone cannot adequately explain the fundamental axial shifts in Asia—the shift from politics to the economy and the shift from decolonization to development—that have characterized the transformation of postwar Asia. Therefore, my aim is to superimpose the shift from decolonization to development—which perhaps holds a far more fundamental significance for Asia—on the traditional picture of Cold War–dominated international politics in Asia. The result will be a three-dimensional blueprint of postwar Asia, and it is within this context that I intend to position postwar Japan. I believe conducting this exercise is the only way to obtain a convincing answer to the question posed at the outset of this prologue.

At the same time, I will also attempt to trace the footprints of postwar Japan as it sought opportunities in Asia—to which Japan is connected by the sea—as well as in the rest of the world. Simply put, the Asian Cold War was a history of hot wars that erupted in the Indochinese and Korean peninsulas within the overall context of the confrontation between the United States and China—the latter occupying the center of continental Asia. In contrast, the other current—the shift from decolonization to development—arose in a region that could be described as "maritime Asia," encompassing Japan and insular Southeast Asia, which subsequently spread to the Chinese continent to cover all of Asia today. To explore Japan's position in this overall picture is also to follow the path taken by Japan as a maritime nation connected to the world by the ocean.

Let us begin our journey with an observation of the 1950s immediately after the end of World War II, when the history of Asia started to shift dramatically.

Notes

1 Nayan Chanda, *Brother Enemy: The War after the War* (San Diego: Harcourt, 1986), 1.
2 Chanda, *Brother Enemy*, 4.
3 Benedict Anderson, *Imagined Communities: Reflections on the Origin and Spread of Nationalism* (London and New York: Verso, 1983), 1.

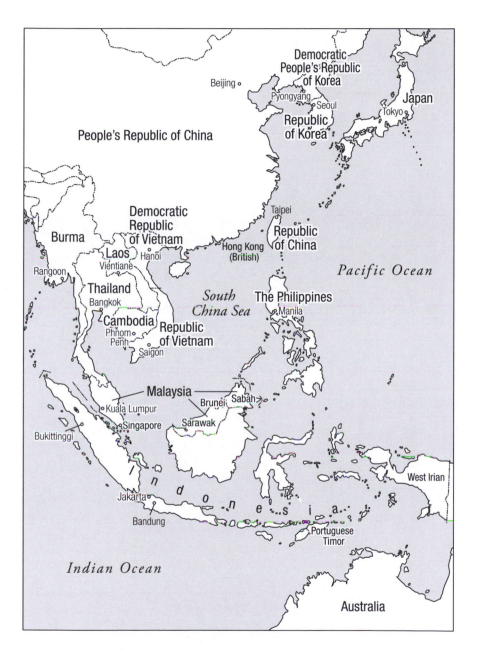

Map of East Asia and Southeast Asia in the 1960s.

1 The birth of "Asia"

The Bandung Conference and Japan's dilemma

Figure 1.1 Chinese Premier and Foreign Minister Zhou Enlai at the podium during the Bandung Conference, April 1955. The man on the left speaking into the microphone at Zhou's side is an interpreter.

Source: © Kyodo News.

The birth of "Asia"

Asia is the stage upon which the events of this book unfold. Yet "Asia" did not actually exist before World War II—at least not in the context of international politics.

Since ancient times, Asia has certainly been a major stage for human civilization and history. However, international politics in its original, modern meaning refers to a world shaped by sovereign nations (though I should note that this very approach to international politics has come under fire and is subject to change). And if we go by that definition, Asia, while it may have served as a "stage" for international politics, could not have been an actor or leader in the process. With only a few exceptions, such as Japan, most of its vast expanse of land had historically been covered by either colonies or spheres of influence set up by the great powers. In the world preceding World War II, "international politics" betrayed its name by remaining the monopoly of a few great powers.

If so, when was "Asia" born into the arena of international politics? With the start of World War II, imperial Japan began its "southward advance" in Asia, disrupting Western colonial domination in its wake. Soon afterward, the Japanese empire met its own destruction and defeat, signaling the end of an era for the Japanese. Yet its downfall signified the beginning of renewed turbulence for Asia. The collapse of domination in its two forms—Western imperialism and military rule under imperial Japan—gave way to an era of independence in Asia, which had long been dominated by powers outside the region.

It was not to be a smooth transition. In Northeast Asia, the overbearing presence of imperial Japan that had been felt throughout the region quickly evaporated upon its defeat. However, disagreement over the process of nation-building became entwined with ideological conflict, plunging both China and Korea into civil wars that ended with the creation of two divided nations. Meanwhile, in Southeast Asia, Western countries that emerged as victors of World War II returned with the intent of reconstructing their colonies, thus setting into motion a protracted process that led to decolonization.

Despite the considerable hardships that accompanied these developments, including civil wars fraught with ideological conflict and battles fought for independence, one after another, sovereign nations emerged on Asian soil. And it was this consecutive creation of numerous sovereign nations that indeed marked the "birth of Asia" in international politics. But was their emergence an event that had any significance for the existing order of "international politics"? After all, they appeared to be a mere cluster of weak emerging nations.

Still, one event led to a broad recognition that both Asia and Africa had made their debut as new actors with considerable significance in the world of international politics—and that was the Asian-African Conference held in 1955, where newly independent states from the two continents gathered in Bandung, Indonesia, to take part in an event known widely as the Bandung Conference.

"Let a new Asia and new Africa be born!" declared President Sukarno of the host country, Indonesia, upon the opening of the Bandung Conference, which was attended by twenty-nine newly independent nations from Asia and Africa that proudly proclaimed their rejection of colonial rule and endorsement of mutual solidarity. For Western nations, it was the first international conference held in their absence. It was a significant event in world history that signaled the end of an era in which international politics had been monopolized by a handful of great powers. The Bandung Conference was indeed a symbol that marked the birth of Asia.

For Japan, this "birth of Asia" meant that by the time it regained its independence through the San Francisco Peace Treaty following the Allied occupation, the Asia that it now encountered had changed beyond recognition from the Asia it had previously known. The Bandung Conference was to be the first international conference attended by Japan since the end of the war, and it was at Bandung that Japan came face-to-face with the newly born Asia for the first time.

As I will examine more closely in Chapter 2, at the time only a few Asian countries had signed the San Francisco Peace Treaty, and Japan was left with the unfinished business of seeking reconciliation with many countries. Postwar Japan was about to take the first step in its return to the international community. How did it face the Bandung Conference and the new Asia that it represented?

> Will Japan cooperate in creating a new destiny for Asia as an independent Asian nation, or will it seek to reap immediate profit as a pawn of Western countries? The answer will be revealed by Japan's behavior at the Bandung Conference.[1]

This was how one Japanese diplomat perceived the attention with which Asia regarded Japan prior to the conference.

The central issues that dominated the Bandung Conference were the burgeoning aspiration for independence and indignation against imperialism, which was still rampant around the world. Should Japan get into line as a part of Asia, or should it place its priority on moving in step with Western countries, which were becoming increasingly alarmed by the rise of nationalism in Asia? For Japan, the Bandung Conference was an occasion that could force it to confront the "either the West or Asia" choice, demanding a definitive answer to the conundrum the country had been grappling with since the Meiji era of modernization. Moreover, the long shadow of the Cold War that engulfed the postwar world was also cast over the conference, constraining Japan's options at every turn.

What were the realities that lay behind Asia in its infancy? And how did Japan determine and choose its position under those circumstances? We will seek out the origins of postwar Japan's engagement with Asia, as it came into sharp focus at the Bandung Conference.

An invitation to the Bandung Conference

It was in late December 1954, two years after regaining independence through the San Francisco Peace Treaty, that Japan received an invitation to the Bandung Conference. The postwar era led by Prime Minister Shigeru Yoshida had run its course, and the invitation came as Japan faced a major turning point.

During the Occupation, Prime Minister Yoshida took pride in the tremendous influence he had gained by forging a special relationship with General Douglas MacArthur, Supreme Commander for the Allied Powers. But Yoshida's star was waning rapidly as the Occupation came to an end, and powerful prewar politicians who had been purged from public office—such as Ichiro Hatoyama, Mamoru Shigemitsu, and Nobusuke Kishi—returned to the main stage of politics. Gaining momentum, the anti-Yoshida camp formed the Japan Democratic Party and finally succeeded in ousting him from power on December 7 with the support of the Japan Socialist Party. This marked the end of Yoshida's extended reign.

The new prime minister was Ichiro Hatoyama, who had been barred from assuming public office in 1946, just as he was about to be elected prime minister as the head of the Liberal Party of Japan. It was Hatoyama who had appointed Yoshida to take his place. There was speculation that Yoshida had promised to hand over the premiership and party leadership to Hatoyama upon his return, but that had not happened. Due in part to this history, the two men became locked in a fierce rivalry. Hatoyama and the anti-Yoshida camp also blamed Yoshida's excessive "cooperation" with the United States for significantly "distorting" Japan's standing.

Having attained the long-coveted position of prime minister, Hatoyama set forth his government's agenda, which consisted of rearmament and constitutional revision as well as autonomy from America in the area of foreign affairs. It also called for a resumption of relations with China and the Soviet Union. Each of these policies strongly indicated his intention of correcting the state of Japan's "distorted" subservience to the United States under the Yoshida administration.

With his cheerful disposition and commoner's touch, Hatoyama enjoyed great popularity among the Japanese people, who were fed up with Yoshida's overbearing political style. In addition to his personality and the sympathy he received for having been purged from public office, Hatoyama was also bolstered by the pent-up sentiment of anti-US nationalism that was simmering in Japan at the time.

While the Peace Treaty had given back Japan's independence, there had been no end to the incidents and accidents occurring at US military bases across the country. And then came the *Daigo Fukuryu Maru* incident in March 1954, in which a Japanese tuna fishing boat was exposed to radioactive fallout from a US hydrogen bomb test on the Bikini Atoll, causing the death of the ship's radio operator. The incident, which was described as the third atomic disaster after Hiroshima and Nagasaki, only reinforced the impression that Japan was somehow still under occupation. Hatoyama's slogan of "autonomy from America" resonated positively with the public sentiment of wanting to escape the overwhelming presence of the United States.

Meanwhile, the international environment surrounding Japan had also begun to change, as if in response to the end of the Yoshida era. Until then, Japan had been confronted by the sharp divisions the Cold War had created in Asia as a result of the Korean War. Cut off from the Chinese continent with which it had enjoyed intimate ties before the war, postwar Japan had no choice but to set off on its path with only half the world that was left to it.

The first signs of change began to appear in 1953, following Stalin's death. The Soviet Union and China shifted their hard-line approach, adopting a more accommodating tone that was described as a "peace offensive" and making overtures to Japan for peaceful coexistence and mutual trade. China in particular had made an impressive debut in the international community, defying the US policy of containment by playing a leading role in the 1954 Geneva Conference, which was held to discuss issues such as restoring peace to Indochina. The Cold War divisions in Asia were beginning to seem less impregnable than before.

In Asia, the Cold War began with the Korean War. For Japan, it generated special demands from the US forces and paved the way for its economic recovery. But a cease-fire was reached in 1953, and by the start of 1954, Japan had slipped into a recession, due in part to the fiscal austerity necessitated by its deteriorating balance of payments. Amid the spread of a pessimistic belief that this spelled the end to its postwar reconstruction, calls for resuming relations with the Chinese continent began gaining strength in Japan.

For the United States, this meant grappling with the growing fear of the neutralization of Japan. Once the ongoing thaw in the Cold War in Asia and rising anti-US sentiment in Japan were joined with its desire to resume trade with China, it was possible that Japan could gradually drift away toward China and the Soviet Union. While things might not go that far, Japan could nevertheless choose the path of non-alignment, as India had done under Prime Minister Jawaharlal Nehru. The emergence of the Hatoyama government, waving its banner of "autonomy from America," seemed to justify such concerns.

The first cabinet formed by Hatoyama, which was to serve primarily as a caretaker government in the wake of Yoshida's resignation, had come into existence with the support of the Japan Socialist Party on the condition that general elections be held within the next three months. Hatoyama needed to win those elections to form an effective government and was pressed to take an original stance. This was the state of affairs when Japan received the invitation to the Bandung Conference.

On one hand, the Bandung Conference, an effort to bring Asia together across the dividing lines of the Cold War, seemed to offer a golden opportunity to demonstrate Hatoyama's policy of autonomy from America. On the other hand, there was no denying that its relationship with the United States was vitally important for postwar Japan. America, meanwhile, was becoming increasingly alarmed at the prospect of a non-aligned Japan and the rise of Asian nationalism. Presented with this situation, what course did Japan eventually choose?

To find out, we must first examine the political circumstances in Asia that led to the Bandung Conference and the reasons that Japan was invited to take part.

Groping about for Asian non-alignment

The Bandung Conference was conceived and realized by countries that were collectively known as the Colombo Group, comprising India, Indonesia, Burma (now Myanmar), Pakistan, and Ceylon (now Sri Lanka). The Colombo Group exerted its presence in the 1950s as a leader of the Asian non-alignment movement, which was rooted in its firm resolve to prevent the Cold War from penetrating into Asia.

The change in Soviet leadership following Stalin's death brought about an easing of global tensions in the Cold War between the East and West; in Asia, too, a conclusion was sought for the Korean War and the conflict in Indochina. However, even as the major powers moved toward détente, there were increasing signs in Asia that the Cold War was about to engulf the entire region.

The US administration of Dwight D. Eisenhower that came to power in 1953 saw the Cold War between the United States and the Soviet Union shifting away from military confrontation toward political and economic rivalry and concluded that maintaining a sound economy and budget was what America needed in order to win. To that end, it adopted a new policy, dubbed the "New Look," in which the United States would focus its resources on the relatively cheaper option of nuclear weapons, while an expanded network of allies would shoulder the burden of maintaining conventional forces. In order to give concrete form to this policy, the United States took the initiative to establish military organizations such as the Southeast Asia Treaty Organization (SEATO), which had members including the Philippines, Thailand, Australia, the United Kingdom, and France, and the Middle East Treaty Organization (METO), which was joined by countries including Iran, Turkey, and Pakistan.

SEATO was to encircle China from the south with the prospective participation of Taiwan, which particularly inflamed the Chinese. In September 1954, as if timed with the final stages of SEATO's formation, China began bombarding the Quemoy islands off the coast of Fujian Province that had come under the control of the Chiang Kai-shek government. This marked the beginning of the First Taiwan Straits Crisis.

The Eisenhower administration became ensnared in the dilemma of not wanting to abandon Taiwan while being equally unwilling to engage in an all-out war with China; the military establishment proposed using nuclear weapons against China. Although the nuclear option was averted in the end, the US–China rivalry began to take on an explosive nature, in stark contrast to the US–Soviet Cold War, which appeared to be settling down to a state of relative stability.

For the newly independent countries of Asia, this meant that the rough waters of the Cold War were now lapping at their very feet. The idea of Asian non-alignment was the product of their anguished hope of avoiding involvement in a Cold War between the East and West that had nothing to with them in the first place. As the central figure of this movement, India's prime minister Nehru offered various peace proposals for the Korean War and the conflict in Indochina, but none of them were ever accepted by the United States. This prompted Nehru to meet with the leaders of countries that shared India's position in Ceylon's capital, Colombo, where they adopted a resolution that was bitingly critical of America's Cold War policies on a possible cease-fire in Indochina and on China's UN membership. The countries that raised their voices on this occasion were subsequently referred to as the Colombo Group.

The Asian-African Conference—later to be known as the Bandung Conference—also had its origins in the Colombo Conference. The idea was first presented by Indonesian prime minister Ali Sastroamidjojo. Underlying his proposal for a gathering of emerging nations from Asia and Africa was the tense situation that surrounded Indonesia at the time.

Indonesia had declared its independence upon Japan's defeat in August 1945, yet it took four more years of bitter fighting against the Dutch—the country's former colonial masters, who had returned after World War II to reestablish their rule—for Indonesia to finally secure its independence. Even then, however, the Dutch retained their hold on West Irian in the western half of the island of New Guinea, and there the struggle against colonialism raged on. For Indonesia, the formation of SEATO signified the emergence of an overpowering anti-Communist military alliance in its vicinity; in particular, the presence of colonial powers within that alliance—the United Kingdom and France—gave rise to an acute sense of crisis. The extent of Indonesia's concern is evident in the fact that discussions took place within the Indonesian government regarding the possibility of forming a mutual non-aggression pact among Indonesia, India, Burma, and China as a countermeasure against SEATO.

No matter how strong its desire to avoid the threatening onslaught of the Cold War or colonialism, the task was beyond the powers of a young nation. Yet, as powerless as they may have been on their own, the newly independent countries of Asia and Africa could establish a foothold if they raised their voices as one. This was the fundamental idea behind the Asian-African Conference.

However, Indonesia's proposal was met with skepticism from the leaders of other countries. For one, such a conference had no precedent, and even if it could be realized, it would be impossible to build a consensus at such a meeting. It was difficult enough deciding which countries to invite. The proposal was met with a series of negative arguments. Sastroamidjojo persisted, however, and the issue was ultimately settled under Nehru's leadership with an expression of "moral support" for the Indonesian proposal. At any rate, the mood at the time was overwhelmingly skeptical toward Indonesia's ability to host such a major international event as it grappled with political and economic instability at home.

Seeing that the key to realizing the conference lay with Nehru, the central figure of the Colombo Group, Sastroamidjojo flew to New Delhi in a bid to win him over. Nehru's lukewarm response had been influenced by India's conflict with Pakistan. In the process of their partition from British India to gain independence, India and Pakistan had experienced a violent religious conflict that left thousands dead. Since then, the two countries had continued to lock horns in a struggle that was suggestive of a familial hatred, including an exchange of fire over their respective territorial claims to Kashmir. Nehru was concerned that, even if they succeeded in hosting an Asian-African Conference, the Muslim countries would have the upper hand in terms of sheer numbers, and with their support Pakistan could seek to undermine his leadership (subsequent events did in fact prove that Nehru had been justified in his concerns).

Still, in the end, Nehru gave his approval to holding an Asian-African Conference. It has been suggested that he did so because the idea generated an unexpectedly favorable reaction within India and because Nehru hoped to demonstrate his support for the Sastroamidjojo government, which was pursuing the same path of non-alignment as India. At any rate, Nehru had changed his mind in support of the conference, and this carried great weight. Burma and Ceylon followed suit and expressed their approval, and the efforts of the Indonesian government finally began to bear fruit.

The realities behind the "Five Principles of Peaceful Coexistence"

The enthusiasm of host country Indonesia was unmistakably the greatest driving force in realizing the Bandung Conference. However, while "Asian-African" was being used as a single phrase, it contained many countries with distinctly different political systems. Most prominent among them was Communist China, which occupied a pivotal position on the Asian continent. There was a need to ensure that the Bandung Conference would indeed be a gathering of "Asian-African" countries that transcended differences in their systems of government, and the essential element in doing so were the "Five Principles of Peaceful Coexistence" proudly championed by Nehru and Zhou Enlai, premier and foreign minister of China.

The Five Principles of Peaceful Coexistence comprised the following tenets: Mutual respect for each other's territorial integrity and sovereignty, mutual non-aggression, mutual non-interference in each other's internal affairs, equality and cooperation for mutual benefit, and peaceful coexistence. At a time when the Cold War between the East and West was escalating, the Five Principles gained recognition for laying out the path to peaceful coexistence between countries with different political systems. To this day, China often refers to these Five Principles as the foundation of its foreign policy.

The Five Principles of Peaceful Coexistence were originally incorporated into the preamble to an agreement signed between China and India in April 1954 concerning the issue of Tibet. The Five Principles began attracting attention, as they were subsequently included in joint statements issued upon Zhou Enlai's visits to countries such as India and Burma. Yet the Five Principles were by no means a set of abstract ideals; they were produced by the raw realities of the political dynamics that governed international relations at the time.

The new China that came into being in 1949 was full of political vigor. "We must always add the word(s) 'genuine' because there are many false independent nations in Asia [where] the heads of puppet regimes follow orders from the headquarters of imperialism." These comments, made by Soong Ching-ling, widely known as one of the "Soong Sisters," were made in December 1949, when she was serving as vice president of China's Central People's Government Council. (Incidentally, Ai-ling, the eldest of the Soong sisters, was the wife of Kung Hsiang-hsi, finance minister of the Nanjing government of the Kuomintang, or the Chinese Nationalist Party, while Ching-ling was the wife of Sun Yat-sen. The youngest of the sisters, May-ling, was the wife of Chiang Kai-shek. The Soong sisters had gone their separate ways over the direction of the Chinese revolution.)

In the early days of its establishment, China's position on the newly independent nations of Asia was strongly colored by class warfare, as it pursued its policy of actively supporting the military struggles of Communist groups that were on the rise in countries such as the Philippines, Malaya, and Burma. Mao Zedong regarded Nehru's India as being a mere tool of imperialist forces.

In contrast, Nehru saw the fundamental nature of the Communist victory in China as the culmination of an agrarian revolution and intended to seek coexistence from the onset. India recognized the new China just two months after its establishment and kept up its hospitable approach, seeking to broker a cease-fire in the Korean War and supporting China's bid to join the United Nations.

This mismatched relationship between China and India took a turn for the better in 1954. Along with the Soviet Union, China shifted its strategy to one of "peaceful coexistence" and participated in the Geneva Conference, which addressed the issue of Vietnam. While the North Vietnamese saw the liberation of the entire nation as being imminent, China applied pressure to restrain their drive, thus achieving a cease-fire in Indochina by temporarily maintaining the country's divided status. Talks to end the tensions between China and India over Tibet were also concluded in April 1954, and an agreement upholding the Five Principles of Peaceful Coexistence was signed. What lay behind China's decision to adopt this accommodating approach?

As previously noted, China in its early years had pursued a policy of actively supporting armed revolution across Asia. But by this time, its efforts had ended in failure, save for some exceptions such as Vietnam. Above all, the Chinese leadership was being confronted with the pressing need to focus on its own nation-building. As soon as it was founded, the young country had been forced to intervene in the Korean War, which had resulted in hundreds of thousands of casualties. Mao's own eldest son was among those killed in the war. Having allocated nearly half its national budget to military spending in 1950 and 1951, China remained incapable of developing its economy. It was now a matter of urgency for the country to secure a peaceful international environment in which to concentrate on reconstructing its battered economy.

In concrete terms, the Five Principles of Peaceful Coexistence amounted to an official declaration by China that it was abandoning its support for revolution in various regions of Asia, which had been a key policy until now. Seemingly obvious phrases such as "mutual non-interference in each other's internal affairs" and "mutual respect for each other's territorial integrity and sovereignty" meant nothing less than the abandonment of its policy of aiding revolution. And for India, Burma, and the others, this premise was indeed the sine qua non for a "peaceful coexistence" with Communist China.

In response to this shift in Chinese policy, Nehru felt the need to bring China deeper into the fold of the international community. In his view, one of the factors prompting Chinese leadership to embrace radical ideology was the isolation it suffered as a result of the US policy of containment. As a neighboring country, it was extremely important for India to keep China firmly on its path of "peaceful coexistence" through international engagement and to ensure there was no relapse. China's participation in the Bandung Conference would offer a unique opportunity for bringing this about.

At the same time, by trumpeting their amicable relationship as a model of "peaceful coexistence," India was seeking to create an environment that would discourage its giant northern neighbor from rekindling the hostile attitude it had taken with India in the past. The intended result was to achieve what could have been described as "containment through friendship."[2]

The Five Principles of Peaceful Coexistence were thus shaped by the ulterior motives of China and India. Yet it was under these same principles that the two major nations formed in postwar Asia overcame the differences in their political systems to build a friendly relationship. And it was on this basis that the Bandung Conference came to be.

Why Japan was invited

In December 1954, the leaders of the Colombo Group gathered in Bogor, southern Jakarta, to discuss concrete plans for co-hosting the Asian-African Conference. The leaders began by deciding on the goals of the coming conference, which included promoting cooperation among Asian and African countries and holding a discussion on colonialism. They also agreed on the principle that participation signified nothing more than a country's support for the goals of the conference and was not meant to affect its relationship with other participating countries.

This was necessary because the ever-darkening shadow cast over Asia by the Cold War meant that some of the countries attending the conference had yet to establish diplomatic relations with each other—as was the case between Japan and China, which I shall discuss later. The organizers sought to keep this from becoming an obstacle for some countries contemplating attendance. The whole purpose of the Asian-African Conference lay in bringing to the same table countries with different political systems that had yet to achieve mutual recognition to encourage better understanding of each other.

However, in spite of this agreed principle, once they reached the point of hammering out the concrete aspects of the conference, the Colombo Group became entangled in a heated debate that reflected the ulterior motives of its members. Deciding on which countries to invite was a particularly thorny issue. It was obvious that the conference would take on a completely different significance and nature depending on which countries were invited to attend.

There was no objection to inviting the fourteen countries Indonesia had approached beforehand, including Egypt, Iran, and Iraq. Next, it was decided that Israel would be left out so as to avoid a backlash from Arab countries. North and South Korea, as well as Mongolia, were also to be taken off the invitation list on the grounds that there were "various political complications" involved. There were also proposals to invite the Soviet Union and Tibet, but they were rejected on the grounds of "excluding controversial issues."

Australia and New Zealand had been approached unofficially; their participation was enthusiastically supported by Pakistan, whose interests lay in cooperating with these countries to provide a counterweight to China and India. Nehru expressed his reservations, however, arguing that they were from another continent, and the two countries were eventually eliminated on the grounds that they had not made an official request to participate.

The discussion came to a head over the pros and cons of inviting China. Of the five countries comprising the Colombo Group, India, Indonesia, and Burma came out in support of inviting China, while Pakistan and Ceylon voiced their opposition, reflecting the sharp division between the three non-aligned countries and the two pro-Western countries. In addition to this rift in ideology, the bitter rivalry between India and Pakistan over such issues as their territorial claims on Kashmir erupted at this point, bringing the talks to a standstill.

The matter was finally settled by Burma's prime minister, U Nu. He told the group that if China was not invited, Burma would decline the position of co-host and refrain from attending the conference altogether. At this, even Pakistan had no choice but to give in, and thus it was decided that an invitation would be extended to China. U Nu had reaffirmed the Five Principles of Peaceful Coexistence with Zhou Enlai upon the latter's visit to Burma and was unwavering in his support for China.

Incidentally, the issue of inviting China was intricately linked to the reason why Japan was also to be invited, even though it was not included in the invitation list originally prepared by India. Pakistan had put forth a powerful plea to include Japan, but Nehru expressed his reservations by pointing out that there were "countries which have unfinished business to settle with Japan."[3] As we shall examine in detail in the next chapter, many Southeast Asian countries had not signed the San Francisco Peace Treaty, and postwar settlements had been left to bilateral negotiations. By that time, Japan had signed a war reparation agreement and a peace treaty with Burma, but negotiations on war reparations with Indonesia and the Philippines had run into difficulties.

Pakistan's prime minister Mohammad Ali Bogra disputed Nehru's argument by bringing up the issue of China: "Speaking of unfinished business, what about Communist China?"[4] At that point, the debate over inviting China had not yet been decided. Including China was Nehru's main concern, and he feared that insisting too strongly that Japan be excluded could lead to a similar decision against inviting China, so he eventually withdrew his opposition to inviting Japan. That marked the decisive moment for Japan. While Indonesia and Burma were two countries deeply involved with Japan, particularly because of the damage they had suffered during World War II, they kept their silence throughout this exchange. Later, however, an Indonesian delegate recalled how their lack of proficiency in the English language worked against Indonesia and Burma, preventing them from making a foray into the acrimonious exchange taking place between India and Pakistan.

What was Pakistan's aim in advocating Japan's inclusion? At the time, Pakistan was struggling desperately to wrest control of the Asian-African Conference away from India and China and their Five Principles of Peaceful Coexistence. India and Pakistan were like twins who were originally intended to gain independence from British colonial rule as a single state. However, in the wake of the religious turmoil that pitted Hindus against Muslims and left as many as a million people dead, they had emerged as two separate states.

Pakistan was divided into its eastern and western regions by India (Bangladesh remained part of Pakistan until its independence in 1971 following the third Indo-Pakistani war). To a country that felt its very existence was in peril, India was an overwhelmingly large neighbor threatening to swallow it whole. In the words of a senior official of Pakistan's Foreign Ministry, "There was no doubt that the policies being pursued by the Indian Foreign Ministry were designed to destroy Pakistan."[5] Accordingly, Pakistan was forced to use whatever resources that were at its disposal to prevent China and India from joining forces and increasing their sway over Asia.

Inviting Japan was an important means to that end. In the event that India advocated inviting China, Pakistan's strategy was to argue for extending an invitation to Japan, "the leading anti-Communist player...[to] prevent the conference from being steered towards a unilateral direction," according to Pakistan's ambassador to Japan.[6] Pakistan was also working to persuade other free-world countries such as Turkey to participate in the conference.

Pakistan's actions, including inviting Japan to the conference, may appear to have been based on its position as a member of the Western bloc, which was seeking to stem the offensive of the non-aligned and Communist camps. By joining both SEATO and METO, Pakistan had also become the only country in Asia that belonged to several anti-Communist military alliances led by the United States. However, the true motivation was Pakistan's desire to stand up to the Indian juggernaut with US backing. Although these actions seemed at first glance to be dictated by the Cold War, their true nature was more of a guise Pakistan put on to attract US attention.

At any rate, Pakistan's invitation to Japan stemmed from its pursuit of a highly focused political agenda. Meanwhile, there was a growing momentum in Japan toward achieving "autonomy from America" immediately following the establishment of the Hatoyama government, and an enthusiastic public hailed the news that Japan had been invited to the Bandung Conference as a "golden opportunity for returning to Asia." Upholding the slogan of "autonomy from America," the Hatoyama government was faced with a potentially incompatible set of options—of either pursuing Japan's goal by seizing the golden opportunity for returning to Asia or playing Japan's expected role as the leading anti-Communist player. Which course did it ultimately choose? To find out, let us first examine the US response, which was to significantly influence Japan's decision.

Asian nationalism—an American headache

The conclusion of talks at Bogor was followed by an announcement that the Asian-African Conference would take place in Bandung, Indonesia, and also included the goals of the conference and the countries that had been invited. (Hereafter, I will refer to this event by its widely known name: the Bandung Conference).

The American response was that this was of no direct concern to them, since the United States was not a member of Asia, nor had it been invited to the conference. Despite such public posturing, however, the Eisenhower administration had in fact become increasingly concerned. There was fear that the Bandung Conference could ignite the deep undercurrent of anti-Western sentiment that flowed throughout the region and give rise to a stronger sense of solidarity among both Communist and non-Communist nations through their identification with "Asia." This could drive a deeper wedge between the Asian countries and the West, which would ultimately benefit the Chinese–Soviet camp.

The Americans believed that Asia harbored a deep resentment against the West rooted in its colonial rule and that once this mood found traction, it could easily unite Asia under an anti-Western banner. "The West, of course, has been dynamic and aggressive and frequently shown a sense of racial superiority; but it also has contributed to human welfare in the realm of technical and material progress," noted US Secretary of State John Foster Dulles, a renowned "Cold Warrior." He was concerned that "if at the conference only the bad things in the record of the West are emphasized it would be easy to give impetus to an 'Asia for the Asians' movement."[7]

It was also a matter of concern for the United States that China, the target of its containment policy, had been invited. By attending the conference, nations friendly to the United States would be directly exposed to China's "Peace Offensive." American unease was further stirred by the highly likely prospect that the conference would be attended by Zhou Enlai, who had demonstrated his exceptional diplomatic skills during the Geneva Conference. Yet if America urged pro-US nations to stay away, it risked them being labeled American "puppets" in Asia, which would inevitably lead to a breakdown in US relations with the host countries of the Colombo Group. It was best that the United States avoid either prospect. In the end, all it could do was to sit back and hope the Bandung Conference would be derailed by developments such as internal discord within the Colombo Group.

At the same time, the United States was also aware that, should the Bandung Conference become unavoidable, it had to prevent the event from leaning toward the non-aligned or Communist camps by having the pro-Western camp be represented by a powerful leader who could confront Zhou Enlai. But for now, the United States would wait and see. It requested its Asian allies, including Japan, to suspend any decisions on their position with respect to the Bandung Conference for the time being.

Against Dulles' expectations, as time went by the conference moved steadily closer to becoming a reality. In late January 1955, having concluded that there was no stopping the Bandung Conference from being held, the US government switched to a policy of requiring pro-US countries to attend the conference and dispatched the following guidelines to each country: Send the "best representative" to participate in the conference; be extra sensitive to Communist countries seeking to manipulate the event; and form an effective united front with other non-Communist countries to foil Communist intentions. In response to this shift in US policy, Japan decided to participate in the Bandung Conference.

Mamoru Shigemitsu—between the Greater East Asia Conference and the Bandung Conference

As Japan began considering its participation in the Bandung Conference, two possible positions had begun to emerge within the Hatoyama government. While Prime Minister Hatoyama and his aides saw Japan's participation in the conference as an opportunity to "return to Asia," Foreign Minister Mamoru Shigemitsu believed Japan should play its part as "the leading anti-Communist player" and live up to the expectations of Pakistan and, above all, the United States.

The difference between Hatoyama and Shigemitsu revolved around their views on Japan's basic foreign policy. Hatoyama advocated autonomy from America and had repeatedly expressed his eagerness to restore diplomatic ties with China and the Soviet Union. Meanwhile, Shigemitsu made it his business to stamp out the flames ignited by Hatoyama's comments. He believed that the baseline of Japanese diplomacy lay in partnering with the United States and the United Kingdom; its relationship with Asian countries should come second, and improved relations with Communist countries should be third.

Shigemitsu became increasingly alarmed by what he considered "amateur diplomacy" in Hatoyama's pronouncements and sought to pursue Japan's partnership with the United States, which he saw as the priority, with respect to the Bandung Conference. This meant not only that Japan itself should actively participate on the basis of its anti-Communist position, but that Shigemitsu also instructed the foreign ministry to consider the possibility of a Japanese initiative to invite all Asian countries, including South Korea and the Kuomintang government of Taiwan, to the Bandung Conference. Perhaps his aim in giving this directive was to strengthen the anti-Communist camp while simultaneously seeking to bolster solidarity within the Western bloc in Asia, which was marked more by discord than unity. However, foreign ministry officials themselves expressed concern that such a proposal carried a significant risk of introducing disruptive issues such as inviting North Korea or Israel, and it was eventually shelved.

In any case, it was an ironic turn of events that found Shigemitsu working on the Bandung Conference as foreign minister. This was the same Shigemitsu who had been most emphatic in stressing the importance of rising Asian nationalism in Japan's foreign affairs before World War II and who had played a central role in promoting the Greater East Asia Co-Prosperity Sphere and the Greater East Asia Conference as foreign minister and minister of Greater East Asia. Some Western observers felt that, after all, the Bandung Conference amounted to realizing the "Asia for Asians" slogan propagated by Japan during World War II and went so far as to calling it the "Second Greater East Asia Conference."

Yet as he prepared for the Bandung Conference, which could have been seen as the culmination of the ideal of Asian liberation he himself had once championed, Shigemitsu remained curiously distant as he insisted on pursuing Japan's partnership with the United States. His attitude was based on the way he perceived Asian-African nationalism solely within the context of the Cold War between the East and West. This was evident in the foreign policy speech he gave to the House of Councilors in January 1955, in which he stated,

> Communist forces are seeking to wreak havoc along the rear battle lines by skillfully manipulating issues such as nationalism and the need for

higher living standards in Asia and Africa...The ultimate outcome of the Cold War depends on which side clinches the final victory on the rear battle lines—democracy or Communism.

For Shigemitsu, then, it was clear that the role Japan should play in the Bandung Conference was that of thwarting the Communist offensive. In that sense, the most significant factor behind the differences in opinion between Hatoyama and Shigemitsu lay in their perception of the Cold War. In Shigemitsu's view, the tide of détente emphasized by Hatoyama merely signified that the frontlines of the Cold War conflict had now moved from those drawn between the United States and the Soviet Union to the "rear battle lines" of Asia and Africa.

In retrospect, the Greater East Asia diplomacy pursued by Shigemitsu during World War II was intended to align Japan's stated war purpose of Asian liberation with that of the Allied Powers—which had been expressed in similar terms in the Atlantic Charter—thereby eliminating any reason for the Japanese empire and the Allied nations to continue engaging in war. At least, according to *The Pacific War and Asian Diplomacy* by Sumio Hatano, Shigemitsu himself was acutely conscious of his intentions as he maneuvered to end the war at the level of principles.

If this was the case, it is possible that in Shigemitsu's mind, Asia during the war existed primarily as a means for Japan to pursue its diplomacy toward the Allied Powers, while in the postwar era Asia served as a stage for the global Cold War. In either case, his main focus was not on "Asia" per se; perhaps therein lies the key to understanding the apparent disparity between Shigemitsu's approach to the Greater East Asia Conference of 1943 and his view of the Bandung Conference.

The real world of international politics had long been an arena where a handful of powerful players, including Western countries and Japan, sought to gain the upper hand through diplomacy while the rest of the world was merely a "stage." Shigemitsu was not exempt from this mentality, even though—or perhaps because—he had been the foremost diplomat of the Japanese empire.

On the other hand, if there was consistency in Shigemitsu's stance from the prewar years through the postwar era, it was his obsession with centralized diplomacy, in which the Foreign Ministry exercised centralized command over diplomacy under his supervision as foreign minister. The other intention behind Shigemitsu's Greater East Asia diplomacy during the war was to wrest the initiative of guiding foreign affairs from the military authorities and reclaim it through a resurgence in diplomacy. It was from his staunch belief in "centralized diplomacy" that Shigemitsu continued to preach the ideal direction of Japanese foreign policy in the postwar period, disregarding even Hatoyama, the prime minister. However, the prewar framework in which the Foreign Ministry was entrusted to execute the diplomatic authority of the emperor was a thing of the past, and Shigemitsu's pursuit of the ideal of "centralized diplomacy" amidst the turbulence of postwar politics was like walking down a path strewn with obstacles that ultimately led to a dead end.

In late March 1955, Hatoyama formed a full-fledged cabinet following his victory in the general elections and immediately made a formal decision to attend the Bandung Conference. But this gave way to muddled maneuvering over who was to represent the Japanese government. Named as one of the candidates, Foreign Minister Shigemitsu remained unenthusiastic throughout, while maintaining that he "would certainly do [his] best if dispatched..."

The Hatoyama administration and the governing Democratic Party were a motley collection of politicians who had only rallied in their mutual opposition to Yoshida; now, with Hatoyama's health in question and an ongoing contest for leadership between the Democratic Party and the Liberal Party ahead of the planned merger between these two conservative parties, the power struggle intensified. Lacking a political base of his own, Shigemitsu found himself standing on increasingly treacherous ground. Efforts to remove him from office had also surfaced. "I clearly sense the mood to oust the foreign minister. Must be in anticipation of Hatoyama's retirement"—thus he had written in his *Memoirs of Mamoru Shigemitsu*, as he realized the risk of being replaced from his post while in Bandung. Even after the war, Shigemitsu had continued to pride himself on being the "emperor's diplomat." Yet within the administration, he was increasingly being seen as an inflexible obstacle.

While the idea of having Hatoyama himself attend the Bandung Conference held sway for a time, in the end the role of representative went to Tatsunosuke Takasaki, a former businessman who was director-general of the Economic Planning Agency. As a close aide to Hatoyama, Takasaki was responsible for the economic aspects of Japan's relationship with Asia, such as negotiating a reparation settlement with the Philippines and participating in Economic Commission for Asia and the Far East (ECAFE). He had been advising the prime minister to take an active interest in the Bandung Conference as an opportunity to advance Japan's economic pursuits in Asia. Takasaki's appointment as representative was a symbolic decision indicating that Hatoyama's policy now formed the mainstream in the run-up to the Bandung Conference.

Meanwhile, countries like India felt it was odd that Japan had chosen the head of the Economic Planning Agency as its representative. After the conclusion of the Bandung Conference, Nehru commented,

> The Japanese delegate was a disappointment...[He] was an expert in economic affairs and not someone who represented Japan politically. Japan was therefore unable to play the role that was naturally expected of it at the conference. This was unfortunate for Japan.[8]

How, then, did Japan behave at the Bandung Conference?

The Bandung Conference begins

The preparatory stages of the Bandung Conference had been marked by discord within the Colombo Group. And on the eve of its opening, news that an Air India flight supposedly carrying Zhou Enlai to Indonesia had exploded in midair sent shock waves far and wide. It was subsequently revealed that Zhou had changed his plans and had not boarded the plane. China expressed strong condemnation of the Kuomintang government in Taiwan as the mastermind behind the plot. (Later investigation revealed that China had become aware that a Taiwanese secret agent had planted a bomb on the plane during its transit in Hong Kong, but had nonetheless allowed the plane to take off and explode. China's aim was to use the opportunity to demand that the British authorities rid Hong Kong of the Kuomintang intelligence units that had established a base there and to obtain excellent material for its propaganda war against the United States and the Kuomintang.[9] Back then, espionage of the kind seen in movies today was very much a reality.) In spite of this incident, the delegates from various countries began arriving in Bandung, including Zhou Enlai, who had escaped the calamity.

On April 18, 1955, the Bandung Conference opened with Sukarno's declaration: "Let a new Asia and Africa be born!" The principal delegates from each country were to discuss the political issues, while committees were set up separately to address economic cooperation and cultural exchange. It was also agreed that a "consensus method" would be adopted throughout the conference, which entrusted the chairman to rule on whether there was general agreement instead of taking a vote. The method was devised to avoid exposing the differences in standpoint among participating countries and thus to prevent the conference from falling apart.

Representatives from each country then gave their speeches. Takasaki also took the podium, stating, "In World War II, Japan, I regret to say, inflicted damages upon her neighbor nations, but ended by bringing untold miseries upon herself... becoming the only people who have experienced the horrors of the atomic bomb," and stressed that "Chastened and free, she is today a nation completely dedicated to peace." He further expressed Japan's determination to contribute to world peace in cooperation with the United Nations. The speech was apparently perceived by the floor as being lukewarm.

Countries that were openly anti-Communist, such as Turkey and the Philippines, gave speeches that strongly condemned Communism, and attention was focused on Zhou Enlai's reaction as he took the podium. Yet Zhou adopted a moderate tone as he addressed the delegates who were expecting him to deliver a hard-line rebuttal. "The Chinese Delegation has come here to seek unity and not to quarrel; to seek common ground and not to create divergences," he said.[10] The moderate line he adopted was in stark contrast to the uncompromising tone of the prepared speech that had been distributed beforehand, and this created a favorable impression on the floor.

However, the latent antagonism that had been simmering reached the ignition point on the third day of the conference. It was set off by comments made by Ceylon's prime minister John Kotelawala. Pointing to the existence of Soviet satellite states such as Hungary and Czechoslovakia, he said: "If we are united in our opposition to colonialism, should it not be our duty openly to declare our opposition to Soviet colonialism as much as to Western imperialism?"[11] Everyone on the floor felt the impact of this figurative bomb and turned their gaze upon Zhou Enlai.

As soon as the session ended, Zhou pointed a finger at Kotelawala, pressing him for an answer: "What do you want, Sir John, by proposing a discussion of that Soviet colonialism? Is that to provoke the People's Republic of China? To split us apart and make the Conference fail?"[12] Kotelawala shot back: "Why do you become angry because of my criticism of the Soviet? ...I mentioned only the relations of the Soviet Union with countries of Eastern Europe...If you had just kept quiet, nothing would have happened."[13] Everyone held their breath. Then Zhou smiled, saying, "Very well, I'll think about it till tomorrow morning,"[14] shook Kotelawala's hand, and left the conference room.

Nobody was more astonished by Kotelawala's remarks than Nehru. When Zhou had left, Nehru asked Kotelawala in an admonitory tone: "Why did you do that, Sir John? Why did you not show me your speech before you gave it?"[15] To this, Kotelawala replied: "Why should I? Do you show me yours before you give them?"[16] Nehru seemed stunned, but soon regained his composure and smiled. And as he burst out laughing, everyone joined in, and the scene was contained. It was the most heavily charged moment of the Bandung Conference, and one that signaled the beginning of the stormy debate that ensued.

As secretary general of the Bandung Conference, Roeslan Abdulgani—whose later positions included that of foreign minister of Indonesia—kept a detailed record of the events and recalled how Nehru's preaching, patronizing attitude was often met with resentment by other Asian leaders.[17] It appears that this sense of discomfort toward Nehru and other Indian government officials was commonly shared by the Indonesian side.

A long, stormy debate concludes the conference

The session resumed the next morning, and as Burmese prime minister U Nu reminded all delegates to show self-restraint, both Kotelawala and Zhou appeared to relax. The conflict seemed to have subsided. However, it was then that Pakistan took up a line similar to that of Kotelawala the previous day and began criticizing the Soviet Union. Turkey expressed its support by proposing a draft resolution that said the conference "condemns all types of colonialism including doctrines resorting to methods of force, infiltration, or subversion." Needless to say, this was an obvious allusion to colonialism under Communism. It was decided that a subcommittee would be set up to explore a possible compromise on this issue.

Next, the principal delegates tackled the issue of "peaceful coexistence," and while the idea was supported by India, China, Indonesia, and others, it was opposed by the pro-Western camp—including Pakistan, Turkey, and the Philippines—which viewed it as part of a "Peace Offensive."

At this point, Japan presented its draft for a Bandung Peace Declaration. The proposal called for respecting the United Nations Charter as an alternative to the Five Principles of Peaceful Coexistence and stressed certain economic and social issues that Japan considered important. However, coming in the midst of a heated exchange that was taking place among countries over the pros and cons of "peaceful coexistence," the Japanese proposal was considered vague and failed to attract much attention.

It was now April 23, yet even on this final day of the conference, the participants remained sharply divided over "peaceful coexistence" and the definition of colonialism, with no prospect in sight for pulling together a final communiqué. Thus compelled by the circumstances, the conference was extended by one day. But the next day brought them no closer to an agreement on the political issues, making it necessary to postpone the closing session by an hour or two.

In the committee deliberating on anti-colonialism, a compromise had been suggested to replace "all types of colonialism" with "colonialism in all its manifestations," but the phrase and its underlying implication of Communist colonialism was met with vehement opposition from Zhou. India sided with Zhou, and the discussion came to a complete standstill. At the very last minute, when a breakdown seemed inevitable, events took a dramatic turn.

The Japanese delegation reported what transpired as follows:

> And so a compromise seemed impossible. But it was then that Zhou—apparently seeking to avoid being blamed for the breakdown and considering it expedient to signal his goodwill toward us by supporting our position—skillfully seized the opportunity to concede and made a sudden allusion to the issue of promoting peace. He said he would take on the difficulties and concede on the issue of creating the draft of the Drafting Committee in the form of a peace declaration, as had been proposed by the Japanese delegate. Thus saved from the brink of collapse, the issue of colonialism was settled at once.[18]

In that unexpected moment, Zhou brought up the Japanese proposal, which had been all but ignored, and declared his support. It was a tactful move in which Zhou expressed his wish to avoid a collapse of the conference by conceding on the issue of colonialism. It also served as a show of goodwill toward Japan, sending a message to the Hatoyama government in response to its stated policy of seeking improved relations with China.

Thus, Japan's peace declaration proposal was given new life through Zhou's support, in a turn of events that was completely unanticipated by the

Japanese; this opened the way for the final communiqué to be expressed in the form of the historic Bandung Declaration. (It should be noted that it was the "declaration" format advocated by Japan that was adopted by the final communiqué, and not the content of its proposal.)

At around the same time, the Drafting Committee, which was seeking to resolve the differences over "peaceful coexistence," had also become dead-locked, and emotions were running so high that Egyptian president Gamal Abdel Nasser, who was chairing the committee, considered the situation beyond compromise and was about to call off the discussion altogether. Alarmed by this development, Secretary General Abdulgani got hold of Conference Chairman Sastroamidjojo and rushed back to the conference room with him. Persuaded by their desperate pleas, the delegates returned to their seats, and after another round of difficult negotiations, a document acceptable to all parties was finally produced.

The closing session was held immediately, and the yet-to-be-typed draft of the final communiqué was approved by applause. Abdulgani wrote of this exciting moment, "All of us heaved a great sigh of relief! We have over-come so many difficulties! We have surmounted the obstacles! We have suc-ceeded!"[19] By the time the conference was declared closed, it was nine thirty in the evening.

First contact with China

Alongside the Bandung Conference itself, a matter that attracted much at-tention, both in Japan and abroad, was whether Japan and China would attempt their first contact since World War II. Under US pressure, postwar Japan had given recognition and established diplomatic relations with the Kuomintang government of Chiang Kai-shek, who had fled to Taiwan, as the legitimate "China," instead of the People's Republic of China. This was to be the first postwar event attended by leaders of both Japan and China.

The first contact between Japan's principal delegate Takasaki and Zhou took place on the first day of the conference in the morning of April 18, in the lobby of the hotel where the delegates were staying. Although it was ex-plained as a chance meeting in which Takasaki and Zhou found themselves next to each other and simply exchanged greetings, it had in fact been a premeditated move discussed by Takasaki and Hatoyama.

The Chinese side also seemed prepared for the encounter, and Zhou offered a suggestion: "In China, we plan to create a simplified version of written Chinese characters. I hear Japan also uses simplified Chinese char-acters. What do you think of having scholars from both countries meet to consider creating the same simplified characters?" The two men promised to hold a more substantive discussion during their stay.

Incidentally, two years later, the Chinese urged Japan to take action on Zhou's suggestion regarding the Chinese characters. The then prime minis-ter Nobusuke Kishi was briefed on the background by a Japanese diplomat who had presided at the Takasaki–Zhou meeting. "Don't waste time on such things!" barked Kishi, and that was the end of the matter, according to Akira Okada's *Secret Stories of Diplomacy*.

Four days after making their first contact, Takasaki and Zhou met for a more intensive discussion. In what was in effect the first face-to-face meeting between Japan and China in the postwar era, Takasaki began by offering words of apology: "I have come here today first and foremost to express our sincere apology for the many inconveniences our country caused your country during the war." Zhou replied with an appeal to move the Sino-Japanese relationship forward:

> The last fifty years are but a short period of time when viewed against the thousands of years of amicable relations enjoyed by Japan and China. We must now give careful thought to how we should maintain the amicable relationship between Japan and China from a long-term perspective.

Zhou went on to question Japan's willingness to resume diplomatic relations with China. In response, Takasaki hinted at the difficulty Japan faced in acting against US intentions, saying: "The Japanese government cannot act on its initiative alone, because Japan has yet to attain complete independence, both economically and politically. However, we do hope to normalize the Sino-Japanese relationship as soon as possible." He went on to point out how the division between China and Taiwan, or the Communist Party and the Kuomintang, posed a major obstacle for Japan, saying, "Is there any way your country, Mr. Zhou, could become united with Taiwan? That is our earnest desire."

Taiwan was a highly sensitive issue for the Chinese side. After a moment of silence, it was Zhou who said, "Mr. Takasaki, you are absolutely right to focus on Taiwan as the problem. We would like to continue this exchange of views, particularly on the issue of our becoming united." The two agreed to meet again three days later.[20]

However, the third meeting between Takasaki and Zhou never materialized. What lay behind the scenes was US pressure. While it sought to contain China, the United States was willing to tolerate Japan and China making contact in Bandung as long as their discussion was confined to issues of trade. As it transpired, Takasaki and Zhou had shown signs of venturing onto political ground by discussing the Taiwan issue in particular, which was the most controversial issue between Japan and China. Foreign ministry officials in the delegation working under Shigemitsu had maintained close contact with the US side, and through collaboration, they ensured that the third meeting was canceled.

Japan was eager to restore its relationship with China, and the Chinese side was seeking to draw Japan closer—even if it meant suppressing memories of the war that must have still been fresh in their minds. Yet they found their intentions hindered by the insurmountable wall of the Cold War that now divided Asia along sharp lines.

The "Discovery" of Afro-Asia

As we have seen thus far, contrary to its popular image of being a forum of Afro-Asian solidarity, in reality the Bandung Conference was for the most part preoccupied with conflicting claims that seemed to have been imported directly from the Cold War, such as the pros and cons of "peaceful coexistence" and the tug-of-war over colonialism under Communist rule. Even the Bandung Declaration, which has been described as the fruition of the "Spirit of Bandung," rejecting the Cold War and defying colonialism, was in fact a compilation of compromises. One such example was the rephrasing of "peaceful coexistence" to "live together in peace"—which is nearly identical to the Preamble to the UN Charter—in an effort to make it more palatable to the pro-Western countries.

On the other hand, no matter how much the arguments were tainted by the Cold War, the conference established the undeniable and lasting fact that the newly independent countries of Asia and Africa had held the first international conference in the absence of Western nations and had made their voices heard in the form of the Bandung Declaration.

As Nehru recalled, what was significant about the conference was that, however intangible, it fostered a sense of community among the leaders of the nations. The leaders shared in the realization that they belonged to a common entity of value and significance in this world.[21]

What Nehru described as the "common entity" was indeed what signified the discovery of "Afro-Asia." While they may have differed on their positions with respect to Cold War ideology, the leaders of the nations that gathered in Bandung had discovered that they were bound by a common destiny that transcended such differences. Specifically, it was their aspiration for independence that had led these Afro-Asian countries to transcend their ideological conflicts and band together.

As for Japan, where did it stand within this context, as it took its very first step marking its "return to Asia"? As we have seen, there was nothing conspicuous about the Japanese presence at Bandung. However, we should not be too hasty in viewing this as the inevitable archetype of Japan's politically low-profile diplomacy in the postwar era.

For example, Foreign Minister Shigemitsu believed it was Japan's responsibility to take an explicitly anti-Communist stand in alignment with US allies such as Pakistan and the Philippines. Had Japan done so, however, the scope of Asia to which it "returned" might have been limited to anti-Communist countries such as the Philippines and South Korea. Moreover, these countries represented regions that had suffered the greatest damage at Japan's hands before and during World War II, where anti-Japanese sentiments ran particularly high.

Meanwhile, détente-minded politicians led by Hatoyama might have been drawn toward the idea of neutrality because they, too, were seeking to maintain a distance from the Cold War. And that would have been a more desirable course in widening the scope of Japan's "return to Asia" to include regions represented by the Colombo Group. Had Hatoyama demonstrated this preference and fallen into line with the likes of Nehru, however, it could have led to a critical deterioration in Japan's relationship with the United States, which already suspected Hatoyama of being a "neutralist."

The ambiguity displayed by Japan during the Bandung Conference was chosen as a means to maintain a balance—or at least to avoid a breakdown—between its desire to "return" to a broad region of Asia across the divisions of the Cold War on the one hand and the necessity of maintaining its relationship with the United States, which had taken on a vital importance for postwar Japan, on the other.

Japan certainly faced a dilemma. Yet upon reflection, we find it was a dilemma that arose precisely because of Japan's tendency to overlook the inevitable conflict in issues that appeared to require an either-or choice: "either Asia or the West"; "either the pro-Western camp or the Communist camp." Had Japan been clear about where it stood with respect to these two issues, the choice would have been an easy one to make, and there would have been no dilemma in the first place. However, postwar Japan moved in the opposite direction, gradually coming around to the idea that its national mission actually lay in "bridging" such dichotomies.

Instead of facing up to Communism as the leading anti-Communist player, Japan would seek to broadly connect with Asian countries through their economies—this was the policy adopted by Japan upon its participation in the Bandung Conference. During the economic discussions that took place on the side as the political debate raged on, Japan actively offered its proposals on topics such as the introduction of a multilateral settlement system. Although the system was intended as a means for invigorating trade within the Afro-Asian region, the participants went only so far as to agree with the proposal on principle, since in reality many countries were still operating under the structural networks that bound them to their former colonial masters. And although the final communiqué also included mutual Afro-Asian technical assistance and requests to the United Nations and the World Bank to take a more active interest in Africa and Asia, these, too, remained within the bounds of generalities.

Meanwhile, Japan was also alert to the danger of nationalistic fervor spilling over into the economic activities of these newly independent countries. Japan's basic idea was to revitalize the Asian economy through a vertical division of labor by connecting Japanese industrial products with Asian resources. It would become difficult to realize this idea once each country began demanding economic independence. However, Asia was still caught up in the legacies of colonial rule, which created all the more reason to persist on a course of independence. So, while Japan sought to broadly connect

Asia across political divisions through economic activity, the conditions that could have made Asia receptive to Japan's vision did not exist at the time.

More than anything, the Bandung Conference was permeated by an over-whelming energy that emanated from the aspirations for independence. As Japanese delegation member Shunichi Kase recalled, "The undercurrent of the Bandung Conference was that of a swelling torrent of anti-imperialist sentiment, and I remember being astounded by the tremendous sense of excitement."[22] The astonishment Kase describes mirrored that felt by Japan—a country that had once itself administered colonial rule—at encountering such excitement.

The Asia that appeared before Japan as it joined the Bandung Confer-ence was a region divided by the repercussions of the Cold War, yet simul-taneously bursting with nationalistic fervor in pursuit of full independence. It was a completely changed world from the Asia that Japan had known before and during the war. Moreover, the war had ended only a decade ago, and everywhere in Asia there were gaping wounds left by Japan that had yet to heal.

Suharto, who succeeded Sukarno as the second president of the Republic of Indonesia, had been a member of the Defenders of the Fatherland (PETA) militia set up by the Japanese Army during its occupation of Indonesia in World War II. He recalled those years as follows:

> Without the fighting spirit and sense of nationalism that were drummed into us at PETA, I think we wouldn't have been able to drive back the Dutch when they returned to re-colonize our country. I am grateful to the Japanese Army in that sense. However, it was my feeling that Japan's military occupation of Indonesia had not been for the 'liberalization of Asia,' but for Japan's own interests.

"Food was requisitioned from the farming villages and many [Indonesians] were sent to the frontlines in Burma and elsewhere. Hundreds of thousands of them never returned to the homeland,"[23] he added.

As we shall see in the next chapter, Japan was still struggling to negoti-ate a settlement with Southeast Asian countries on war reparations (at the time of the Bandung Conference, it had managed to conclude an agree-ment only with Burma, in 1954). Under these circumstances, what leads did Japan follow as it sought to make its way into this new region that Asia had become?

Notes

1 Diplomatic Record of the Ministry of Foreign Affairs of Japan.
2 George McTurnan Kahin, *The Asian-African Conference, Bandung, Indonesia, April, 1955* (Ithaca, NY: Cornell University Press, 1956), 8.
3 "Memorandum on the Asian-African Conference," dispatch from Minister Wajima at the Japanese Embassy in Indonesia, to Minister of Foreign Affairs

Shigemitsu, January 11, 1955, based on comments made by the Vice Foreign Minister of Pakistan, Diplomatic Record of the Ministry of Foreign Affairs of Japan, B'0049.

4 Ibid.

5 "Reference material on the Asian-African Conference (11)," based on comments made by the Deputy Vice Foreign Minister of Pakistan, Diplomatic Record of the Ministry of Foreign Affairs of Japan, B'0049.

6 "Reference material on the Asian-African Conference," Asian Affairs Bureau First Division, based on comments made by the Pakistani Ambassador to Japan, February 8, 1955, Diplomatic Record of the Ministry of Foreign Affairs of Japan, B'0049.

7 "Memorandum of a Conversation, Department of State, Washington, April 9, 1955," *Foreign Relations of the United States (FRUS), 1955–1957*, vol. 21.

8 Dispatch from Ambassador Nishimura at the Japanese Embassy in France to Minister of Foreign Affairs Shigemitsu, May17, 1955, private memo from Nehru to Ambassador Malik at the Indian Embassy in France, based on comments made by Malik, Diplomatic Record of the Ministry of Foreign Affairs of Japan, B'0050.

9 Steve Tsang, "Target Zhou Enlai," *China Quarterly* no. 139 (September 1994).

10 "Communist China's behavior at the Asian-African Conference," Asian Affairs Bureau Second Division, May 2, 1955, Diplomatic Record of the Ministry of Foreign Affairs of Japan, B'0050.

11 Roeslan Abdulgani, *The Bandung Connection: The Asia-Africa Conference in Bandung in 1955* (Singapore: Gunung Agung, 1981), 116–117.

12 Ibid.

13 Ibid.

14 Ibid.

15 Ibid.

16 Ibid.

17 Ibid.

18 "About the heated discussion regarding New Imperialism," dispatch from Wajima to Minister of Foreign Affairs Shigemitsu, April 26, 1955, Diplomatic Record of the Ministry of Foreign Affairs of Japan, B'0049.

19 Abdulgani, *The Bandung Connection*, 161.

20 "Minutes of the Takasaki-Zhou meeting," April 22, 1955, Diplomatic Record of the Ministry of Foreign Affairs of Japan, A'0133.

21 "Impressions of the Bandung Conference by delegations: by W.R. Crocker, Australian Ambassador to Djakarta, June 8, 1955," The National Archives of the United Kingdom (Kew) (hereafter TNA), FO371/ 116985 D2231/ 365.

22 Shunichi Kase, *Kase Shunichi kaisoroku* [Memoirs of Shunichi Kase], vol. 1 (Tokyo: Yamate Shobo, 1986), 115.

23 "Watashi no rirekisho: Suharuto (5)" [My Personal History: Suharto (5)], *Nihon Keizai Shimbun*, (January 6, 1998).

2 Japan's "southward advance" and its repercussions

Between independence and the Cold War

Figure 2.1 Prime Minister Nobusuke Kishi with Prime Minister Jawaharlal Nehru of India during Kishi's visit to India in May 1957.
Source: © AP/AFLO.

Confronting the scars of war

At the Bandung Conference, Japan sought to distance itself from the ideological conflict of the Cold War and pursue a path that would enable it to "return to Asia" by focusing on the economy. However, Bandung proved to be yet another reminder for Japan of the impregnability of the thick wall created by the Cold War that stood between itself and the Chinese continent, with which the Japanese had enjoyed such intimate ties in the past. Where, then, was Japan to find new opportunities? Cut off from Northeast Asia, Japan redirected its energies toward Southeast Asia, in what eventually amounted to a "southward advance" by postwar Japan.

Needless to say, Southeast Asia had also come under the shadow of the Cold War. In Vietnam, where France had given up hope of reestablishing colonial rule, the ideological line that split the country into north and south was to become the front line of the Cold War in Asia, culminating in the Vietnam War. Across Southeast Asia, in places such as Malaya and the Philippines, Communist parties had escalated their armed struggle and were engaged in constant warfare with the government or colonial authorities.

On the other hand, there were neutral countries such as Indonesia and Burma, which were part of the Colombo Group, while the British still maintained colonies in Malaya and Singapore. Compared with Northeast Asia, where the dividing lines of the Cold War were sharply defined from the Korean Peninsula to the Taiwan Straits, the situation in Southeast Asia was vastly more complicated in its dimensions. And that was where Japan saw its point of entry.

America gave further encouragement to Japan's interest in the region. While it was heavy-handed in the way it sought to keep Japan and Communist China apart based on its Cold War logic, the United States actively encouraged Japan's advance into Southeast Asia. Again, its motives lay in the Cold War. The Americans concluded that one of the reasons that the now-independent Japan seemed to navigate toward China and the Soviet Union—or toward neutrality—was the lingering memory of its past economic ties with the Chinese continent and that it would be difficult to suppress Japan's impulse toward neutralization unless it finds an alternative market and supply base for raw materials elsewhere. And this was where Southeast Asia came into the picture.

According to the US vision, Japan was to achieve economic recovery by combining its industrial capabilities with the material resources of Southeast Asia, which would simultaneously resolve the shortage of goods in the region and eliminate the social insecurity that had encouraged the spread of Communism. If this plan were to succeed, Japan and Southeast Asia would both achieve economic recovery and become a powerful bulwark against Communism, at no cost to the United States.

At times referred to as the "Marshall Plan for Asia," this idea was repeatedly discussed within the US administration, but was ultimately shelved. Dwight D. Eisenhower, who became president in 1953, emphasized fiscal discipline and market principles; he believed economic recovery should be achieved through trade. Congress was also reluctant to extend large-scale foreign aid. Even though it was never realized, the US plan attracted much attention in Japan in the 1950s, and the idea of "Southeast Asian development" captured people's interest.

However, Southeast Asia was a region upon which Japan had imposed its will during World War II under the Greater East Asia Co-Prosperity Sphere, a region that had been forced to provide manpower and resources, where fierce battles had taken place. Unsurprisingly, memories of the war were still raw in people's minds, and postwar settlement would be an unavoidable issue if Japan wished to reconstruct its relationship with the region. In spite of this fact, Japan had yet to make peace with many Southeast Asian countries under the San Francisco Peace Treaty and had not even established diplomatic relations with many of the countries at the time. As it harbored hopes of a southward advance into Southeast Asia, Japan was confronted by yet another wall in addition to the Cold War—that of its negative legacy from World War II.

But why did so many Asian countries disengage from the San Francisco Peace Treaty? The United States, which led the peace process, had initially planned to take a harsh, punitive stance against Japan. To prevent Japan from becoming a threat in future, certain limitations were placed on its industries, and excess industrial facilities were to be handed over to the Allied nations. As the Cold War intensified, however, America grew more convinced that an excessive weakening of Japan would not only increase its own burden, but would also be a disadvantage from the standpoint of strengthening the pro-Western camp. With the outbreak of the Korean War, the United States renounced reparations claims against Japan at the San Francisco conference and sought approval from other countries.

But the move was met with vehement protest from countries such as the Philippines, which had suffered tremendous damage at the hands of the Japanese during the war. Thus, it was decided that, as an exception, countries that had been occupied by Japan would be given the right to claim reparations. At the same time, it was also agreed that Japan would pay these reparations not in cash, but in the form of services such as the provision of goods and the construction of facilities. Compared to cash payments, the provision of services was more likely to generate demand for Japanese companies. Two countries sought reparations from Japan under these terms: the Philippines and South Vietnam.

What became of Japan's relationships with the other countries that made up most of Asia? China, which was the greatest victim of the war, was in the midst of a civil war at the time, and neither the Chinese Nationalist Party nor the Communist Party was invited to participate in the San Francisco conference. India was critical of the leading role played by the United States and the United Kingdom in the peace talks, and Burma expressed its discontent with the reparations, which led both countries to absent themselves from the talks. And while the Indonesian government signed the Peace Treaty, ratification was denied by its parliament due to dissatisfaction that the reparations were limited to services. As such, the San Francisco Peace process was highly inadequate with respect to Japan's relationship with Asia.

In subsequent negotiations that took place on an individual basis, India renounced its claim, as did China's Nationalist government, which had fled to Taiwan. Cambodia and Laos followed suit and received economic assistance in the form of grant aid as an alternative to reparations. In the end, Japan was to engage in substantial negotiations on reparations with the Philippines, Indonesia, Burma, and South Vietnam—incidentally, countries that were also targeted for its southward advance. Thus, the resolution of the reparations issue presented Japan with the first obstacle in its southward advance.

Overcoming the hurdle of reparations talks

Negotiating the reparations was a daunting task— and understandably so, considering that discontent with the reparations issue had caused so many Southeast Asian countries to withdraw from the San Francisco peace talks in the first place. Once negotiations began, it quickly became apparent that there was an enormous gap between the amount of reparations envisaged by Japan and that demanded by Southeast Asian countries. For example, Indonesia initially demanded US$17.5 billion in reparations—an amount that exceeded Japan's gross national product at the time—while the amount proposed by Foreign Minister Katsuo Okazaki upon his trip to Indonesia in 1953 was US$125 million, less than a hundredth of Indonesia's demand.

In addition, there was an underlying gap in perception between the Japanese side and the Southeast Asian side regarding the nature of the war itself. A deep-rooted perception held by the Japanese side was that to begin with, Japan had fought a war against the United States and European countries and not against the countries of Southeast Asia, which had been under colonial rule at the time. Japan may have lost the war, but its war purpose of "liberating Asia" had been right—perhaps this was the perception implicit in such a view.

Why then, should Japan pay these reparations? Prime Minister Yoshida's response was that reparations were "an investment of sorts." Meanwhile, an official at the Ministry of International Trade and Industry responsible for the reparations issue put it more bluntly. In economic terms, Southeast Asia was to Japan "virgin territory swept by gale-force winds of exclusive nationalism and suspicion toward an invading Japan. What better way to make a safe entry into such an environment than to do so under the pretext of reparations?"[1] Thus, in Japan at the time, the reparations issue was viewed as a means of advancing into Southeast Asia, rather than as atonement for its wartime deeds.

The argument that reparations would ultimately benefit Japan was emphasized in part to convince the Japanese public, which remained in doubt about paying reparations to Southeast Asia. In turn, such words and attitude drew fire from the Southeast Asian side, often derailing progress in the negotiations.

While the going was at times tortuous, the prolonged negotiations on reparations did come to a conclusion, one after another, in the latter half of the 1950s. Agreements were reached with Burma in 1954, the Philippines in 1956, Indonesia in 1958, and South Vietnam in 1959. This was partly due to changes in leadership as well as the changing circumstances in which these countries found themselves, as we shall see later on.

The conclusion of the reparations issue led to a normalization of relations with these countries, and since the reparations took the form of products and services instead of cash payments, it also meant that Japanese companies would be paid by the government to export their products and undertake construction projects in the recipient countries. For Japanese companies, this provided a unique bridgehead for making inroads into the Southeast Asian market. It was also a low-risk business in which payment was guaranteed by the government. And as politicians and influence peddlers became involved, various allegations involving vested interests and collusion emerged.

In one of the episodes that played out in those days, President Sukarno of Indonesia, while being entertained by a Japanese trading company at a hostess bar in Akasaka, Tokyo, became attached to a nineteen-year-old woman named Naoko Nemoto. She would eventually move to Indonesia and become Sukarno's third wife. "Madame Dewi," as she came to be known, became an influential figure in Indonesia's relationship with Japan and in Sukarno's "palace politics."

Yet another aspect of reparations was the fact that compensation to individuals and cash payments were excluded from the reparations, which were mostly allocated to the construction of industrial facilities in the recipient country. This certainly made it difficult for individual victims to appreciate the payments as Japan's compensation for the war.

Such problems inherent to Japan's reparations would persist over the years. Yet if the Bandung Conference had served merely as the first contact between postwar Japan and the other countries of Asia, the reparations issue marked the true beginning of relationship-building. And considering that resumption of diplomatic relations did not come about until 1965 for South Korea and 1972 for China, Japan's relationship-building in Asia began in the south, with Southeast Asia.

This southward advance by postwar Japan, which began with its reparation payments, is usually explained within the context of Japan's economic advance into Southeast Asia. In that respect, Japan was a completely non-political presence, committed solely to economic activity. However, just as Japan was expected to take the role of the leading anti-Communist player at the Bandung Conference—which it had attended seeking a "golden opportunity for returning to Asia"—whether it liked it or not, Japan could never be anything but a political figure in Asia's postwar international politics.

Seen from this broader perspective, its southward advance signified that Japan, which had exited the scene upon its defeat in war, had now reemerged to resume its march into Southeast Asia in full force. And this had the effect of bringing a new dynamism to the situation in Southeast Asia, where the tides of the Cold War, nationalism, and decolonization chased each other. Let us examine the significance of this development.

Groping around in the fluid circumstances of Southeast Asia

Compared to Northeast Asia, the mixed presence of neutralist countries and colonies added multiple dimensions to Southeast Asia, and this kept the region in a constant state of flux.

Northeast Asia had been divided from end to end, between Communist China and North Korea on one side and the pro-Western camp of South Korea, Taiwan, and Japan on the other. But at the same time, the unalterable nature of the situation itself also led to stability. It is ironic that even after the end of the global Cold War, the dividing line that runs from the Korean Peninsula to Taiwan has persisted to this day in a remarkable demonstration of stability.

In contrast, the massive scale of the changes that swept over Southeast Asia becomes clearly apparent by simply comparing a map of the region in the 1950s to one in the present. In the map of the 1950s, Vietnam exists as two countries, one in the north and the other in the south. Singapore, Malaya, and the northern region of Borneo are British colonies, while the western half of New Guinea remains under Dutch colonial rule.

Looking at this map half a century later, we find that Vietnam has long been unified. And while the last remaining Western colony disappeared in 1997 with the return of Hong Kong, the map also shows East Timor, which became the latest country to gain independence in 2002 by breaking away from Indonesia, impressing upon us that the times have indeed come full circle. Above all, Southeast Asia has transformed itself from a mixed bag of neutralist countries, pro-Western countries, and colonies of West European countries into the most highly integrated region in Asia under the Association of Southeast Asian Nations (ASEAN). No other region in the postwar world has undergone such dramatic change.

Why was there so much change and volatility in Southeast Asia after World War II? The events that took place in the half-century after the war represented the very process of Southeast Asia's development as a collective entity of independent nations.

In Northeast Asia, national entities concentrated within territories that roughly correspond to present-day borders had existed for several hundred years, at least since the Qing Dynasty (which lasted from 1644 to 1912)—though they may not have been true nation-states in the modern sense. In contrast, the entire region of Southeast Asia, with the exception of Thailand, was subjected to colonial rule by Western powers for a prolonged period.

Consequently, the extended period of colonial rule had a decisive impact on fundamental issues in Southeast Asia, such as the basic nature of its societies and the boundaries defining independent nations. For example, even though they were both rooted in the Malay culture, Indonesia and Malaysia became two separate countries because they had been colonized by different Western powers—Indonesia by the Dutch and Malaysia by the British. Also, British Malaya (today's Malaysia) was transformed into a multicultural society that included ethnicities besides the indigenous Malays, as a result of the mass influx of Chinese and Indian workers who had been brought in to mine tin and other minerals.

Though it appeared impregnable and everlasting, colonial rule was abruptly crushed by the Japanese army when World War II broke out. This left a substantial impact, but did not mean the end of colonialism. Following Japan's defeat, the Western powers returned to rebuild their colonies as if to reclaim a natural right. And it was the refusal of the colonies to let this happen that set the wheels of history turning toward independence and decolonization.

Decolonization, by its very nature, is not something that can be accomplished in an instant by a specific formal event at a specific point in time, such as a declaration of independence. It is about meeting the challenges of creating a nation and a people out of the prolonged period of colonization, and determining the substance with which to fill the newly independent nation, and the extent to which the influence of the former master should be dispelled. For Southeast Asia, the process involved an ongoing quest for answers that continued to unfold throughout the 1950s and 1960s, overlapping precisely with the postwar period. And this was the fundamental cause of the continuous volatility that afflicted the region in the postwar era.

The process of decolonization became readily aligned with the Cold War conflict on the global stage through the choice of a regime—taking the path of either Communism or capitalism—for building a nation after independence. Conversely, we could also say that the postwar ideological conflict of the Cold War, which was supposedly characterized by stability, was converted into a hot war in Southeast Asia as it became bound up with the dynamic energy of decolonization.

It was none other than this fundamental energy of decolonization that served as a trigger and drew Japan southward in its "return to Asia." One country that came into particular focus was the "anchor" of maritime Asia—Indonesia.

Indonesia—The "anchor" of maritime Asia

There were two epicenters that caused volatility and drove transformation in postwar Southeast Asia. One of these was Indochina and the developments centered in Vietnam. France's retreat from Vietnam was followed by a face-off between the United States and Communist forces that eventually led to the Vietnam War; the region remained a focal point not only for Asia, but for postwar international politics as a whole. Would an American defeat really lead to a "domino effect" of Communist expansion? Would excessive intervention plunge the United States into a bottomless pit of debilitation? It is not difficult to imagine that the outcome of the Vietnam War was seen as having a decisive impact on the future of Southeast Asia.

While it was far less in the public eye than the developments in Vietnam, the other epicenter that nevertheless continued to exert a comparable impact on the region was Indonesia, which was, as described above, the "anchor" of maritime Asia.

Comprising nearly half the territory and population (220 million as of 2006) of the region, Indonesia was the dominant country in Southeast Asia;

its vast size placed it in the realm of the likes of the United States, Soviet Union, China, and India. Other factors, too, added to Indonesia's influence, such as its abundant natural resources—including oil—and its geopolitical importance as the strategic nexus between the Pacific Ocean and the Indian Ocean.

Yet, more than its scale as a nation, what made Indonesia the regional anchor was the path it chose to follow, which had a decisive impact on the political baseline of the region.

We should recall that Java, the island that lies at the heart of Indonesia, had since ancient times been a major center of maritime civilization in Southeast Asia. Indonesia, which was eventually colonized along with Java to form the Dutch East Indies, was also the unrivaled leader with respect to the rise and development of modern nationalism in the region. After World War II, Indonesia engaged in violent conflict to win its independence from the Dutch (though the two countries fought against different enemies, some have observed the similarity between Indonesia and Vietnam and the mutual sense of intimacy between the two countries) and went on to host the historic Bandung Conference. These were accomplishments that further enhanced Indonesia's self-image as the global leader of nationalism and anti-colonialism in the Third World, as personified by President Sukarno, the hero of Indonesian independence.

Consequently, Indonesia took a completely different approach compared to neighboring countries that maintained close ties with their former colonial masters, such as the Philippines with the United States and Malaysia and Singapore with the United Kingdom. Those countries and their previous colonizers were to continuously feel the pressure—both overt and covert—emanating from Indonesia, a major nation proudly advocating nationalism and anti-colonialism. Should a country maintain its bond with its former colonizer after gaining independence, or should it seek to completely discard such ties in order to declare itself truly independent? The direction taken by Indonesia under Sukarno was a significant element that influenced the quest for decolonization in Southeast Asia in the postwar era.

Sukarno pursued a policy of radical nationalism by confronting the colonialist forces, targeting the Netherlands first and then the United Kingdom, ultimately withdrawing from the United Nations and standing against the United States by forging a "Beijing–Jakarta Axis" with China. That alliance lasted until 1965, when it fell apart in the wake of the aborted coup d'état known as the September 30 Incident. Sukarno was replaced by Suharto, whose government was led by the military establishment; his overriding imperative was to pursue anti-Communism and economic development in cooperation with Western nations. Under Suharto, Indonesia went on to become the undisputed leader of the newly created ASEAN.

It was only because of this dramatic transformation of Indonesia, which occupied a central role in the region, that Southeast Asia was able to progress from a period of political activity—characterized by revolution, nationalism, and war—to a period of economic activity that spread development and economic growth throughout the region, which continues to this day. As we follow Indonesia's trajectory from hosting the Bandung Conference to forming the Beijing–Jakarta Axis and becoming the leader of ASEAN, we can easily see how these changes had a significance and influence that went far beyond a single country, exerting a major impact on the regional order.

Furthermore, it was on Indonesia that Japan set its sights as the main destination of its southward advance. As we shall see later, Japan was to achieve its goal by remaining intimately involved with Indonesia throughout the Sukarno years of anti-colonialism as well as in the Suharto years, when development was the overriding priority. Japan's close ties with Indonesia eventually transcended the bilateral relationship and propelled Japan, willing or no, into playing a key role in the struggle to establish order in Asia. Japan's involvement would go on to have a crucial significance in the rising tide of "decolonization to economic development" that was to become the main trajectory followed by postwar Asia.

To begin with, let us shed light on Japan's reparations to Indonesia, which set the precedent, and explore the significance it had for international politics in Asia that extended well beyond that of a bilateral postwar settlement.

Kishi and Sukarno strike a surprise deal

In November 1957, during a visit to Indonesia that took place in his tour of Southeast Asia, Japanese Prime Minister Nobusuke Kishi struck a deal with President Sukarno on the long-standing issue of reparations. Japan agreed to pay a total of approximately US$800 million in reparations and loans combined to Indonesia, which was—along with the amount paid to the Philippines—one of the largest sums Japan paid in war reparations. It had taken twelve years to conclude the negotiations.

As mentioned before, since Indonesia was not a signatory to the San Francisco Peace Treaty, the issue of reparations had been left to bilateral negotiations. The two sides could not agree, however, on the amount of reparations to be paid. The Japanese side eventually adopted the posture of waiting it out until Indonesia softened its stance. Moreover, Japan was simultaneously conducting negotiations with the Philippines, Indonesia, and Burma and had already decided that it would pay reparations on a four-to-two-to-one ratio with respect to these countries. Japan therefore felt it could not make an exception for Indonesia by taking an accommodating stance.

Irritated by Japan's posturing, in June 1954 the Indonesian government demanded that its outstanding debt on trade with Japan be cancelled as part of the reparations, while at the same time imposing tough restrictions on entry and stay by Japanese nationals and on port calls by Japanese ships. These measures further jeopardized the progress of the negotiations.

However, the situation began to change gradually. Even after achieving independence, crucial parts of Indonesia's main industries remained in Dutch hands, and there were growing hopes that Japanese reparations would replace Dutch capital. Meanwhile, Japan had concluded an agreement with the Philippines in May 1954, which created momentum in support of completing the talks with Indonesia.

The Japanese side began to take an active interest in the issue after Nobusuke Kishi became prime minister in February 1957. Meanwhile, in Indonesia, President Sukarno—who had been elevated to a largely symbolic status under the parliamentary cabinet system in spite of his consistent position as president since the nation's independence—finally established a real hold on political power. Spurred by the emergence of forceful leaders who shared a keen interest in settling the reparations issue, negotiations between Kishi and Sukarno were finally concluded in November 1957.

Yet, even as an agreement was reached, Indonesia was in fact facing its biggest crisis since gaining its independence. Sukarno's enemies had launched a major insurgency, and the United States had seized the opportunity to interfere—maneuvering to bring down the Sukarno government, which appeared to be leaning toward Communism. The situation threatened not only to destroy the Sukarno government, but to lead to the disintegration of Indonesia as a nation.

Why did Kishi decide to pay the reparations to Sukarno under these circumstances? And did America look the other way? The issue of Japan's reparations to Indonesia took on greater significance than would ordinarily have been expected of such negotiations.

The threat of Indonesian disintegration

The crisis in Indonesia had its origins in the inherent structural disparities that existed between Java and the other islands. Indonesia consists of as many as 13,000 islands; its population amounts to nearly half that of Southeast Asia as a whole. Almost half of its enormous population is concentrated on the island of Java, which accounts for only 7 percent of its land. Since ancient times, Java had been a major center of civilization in Southeast Asia and remained at the heart of Indonesia even under Dutch colonial rule. This is vividly illustrated by the way all the islands other than Java are collectively referred to as the "Outer Islands" in Indonesia.

Upon its founding, the country had by no means taken a Java-centric stance, as demonstrated by its official national motto, "Unity in Diversity." And yet the idea of a federal system of government, which would have been optimal for a country as diverse as Indonesia, had taken on a negative association in the course of the nation's struggle for independence. When the war of independence ended in 1949, Indonesia was founded as a federal republic through its agreement with the Dutch, whose intentions of maintaining pockets of pro-Dutch forces in some of the self-governing states were quite obvious. After establishing sovereignty, Indonesia hastened its transition to a unitary republic to thwart the aims of the Dutch; thus, the idea of a federal system became stigmatized as a form of government that threatened the independence and unity of the country.

But even as it became a unitary republic, in Indonesia it was said that Dutch colonialism had gone and Javanese imperialism had arrived, as the Javanese—with their overwhelming influence in terms of population, economy, and culture—filled major posts in both central and local governments, and Java was evidently favored as the target of various government measures. On the other hand, most of the resources, including oil and rubber, that were earning foreign currency for the country, were located in smaller islands such as Sumatra. This led to growing discontent among the Outer Islands that the wealth generated by their resources was being used solely for Java's benefit.

With all this in the background, the army centralized its command in a move that was long overdue. As a result, regional armies that had established themselves as localized military factions since the war of independence decided to revolt. One after another, they rushed to seize the administrative control of each state. This movement was joined by influential politicians from the Outer Islands, who demanded a reform of central government, only to be turned down. In February 1958, dissident forces sharing a common discontent against the central government finally declared the establishment of the Revolutionary Government of the Republic of Indonesia in Bukittinggi, in the central region of Sumatra. Local discontent had grown to the point of forming a separate government from the one in Jakarta.

The United States, under President Eisenhower, saw this as an opportune moment to intervene. Fearing that the war of independence could fall into a quagmire and invite a Communist takeover, America had originally sided with Indonesia and had even pressured the Dutch to recognize Indonesian independence. However, the path subsequently taken by Indonesia did not live up to US expectations. The pro-US moderate Islamic government on which America had pinned its hopes proved short-lived; since the formation of the Sastroamidjojo cabinet in 1953, Indonesia had been pursuing significantly leftist diplomatic policies with non-cabinet support from the Communist Party, seeking to strengthen ties with China and the Soviet Union and hosting the Bandung Conference.

Furthermore, in the general elections held in 1955, the Communist Party surpassed pre-election forecasts, making impressive gains that placed it among the four major political parties. The Communist Party went on to win a further victory in the series of local elections that took place in Java in 1957, capturing more than 30 percent of the votes. American authorities became alarmed at the probability that voters in Indonesia—or Java at least—would put communists in power in the near future.

From the US point of view, the most important region in Indonesia was the island of Sumatra, a major oil-producing region whose shorelines form part of the Strait of Malacca. To prevent it from falling into Communist hands, even the idea of dismantling Indonesia and cutting off Sumatra seemed to be an effective measure. Secretary of State Dulles remarked that "between a territorially united Indonesia which is leaning and progressing toward Communism and a breakup of that country into racial and geographical units, I would prefer the latter." The United States had learned a hard lesson from having "lost" China in its entirety to the Communists through its determination to maintain Chinese unity during the civil war between the nationalist government and the Communist Party.

In that sense, it was just as well for the United States that the insurgency was centered in Sumatra. By fall of 1957, America had decided to support the insurgents and began covertly supplying arms and funding through the Central Intelligence Agency (CIA). As we shall see later on, when the central government in Jakarta eventually launched a military offensive to quell the insurgency, America countered the move by conducting air raids from the Philippines and Malaya. Meanwhile, the nationalist governments of Taiwan and South Korea aligned themselves with the anti-Communist cause and offered active support to the insurgents in Indonesia by airlifting arms and providing pilots.

For their part, dissident forces in Indonesia that had originally called for decentralization began to seek further US backing by emphasizing that the aim of their insurgency was to defeat Communism. In response, the United States began to consider recognizing the insurgents as the legitimate government of Indonesia and repealing its recognition of the central government in Jakarta headed by President Sukarno.

Meanwhile, in Jakarta, Sastroamidjojo and his cabinet had lost control of the situation; following his resignation, Sukarno declared martial law throughout the country. Bypassing political parties to provide direct leadership in the succeeding cabinet, Sukarno moved beyond his symbolic status as president to seize actual political power. The crisis faced by Indonesia from the second half of 1957 to the first half of 1958 coincided perfectly with the period during which Japan and Indonesia rapidly developed closer ties. Prime Minister Kishi's visit to Indonesia and the conclusion of reparation talks took place in November 1957, followed by Foreign Minister Aiichiro Fujiyama's visit to Indonesia in January of the following year for the signing of a peace treaty and an agreement on reparations that came into effect in April. What lay behind this rapid development of intimacy in the midst of the crisis? Let us examine the reparation negotiations in detail.

"Let us sip each other's blood in a vow of brotherhood..."

Japan had decided it would pay reparations on a four-to-two-to-one ratio to the Philippines, Indonesia, and Burma; as previously discussed, the main reason its reparation talks with Indonesia had become deadlocked was the latter's insistence on being paid the same amount as the Philippines. Negotiations resumed only after Kishi became prime minister; under discussion was an agreement that had Japan paying US$400 million in reparations, with an additional US$400 million pledged as economic aid to ensure that the actual amount would equal that of the Philippines.

The final political decision that would conclude the negotiations was made in November 1957, while Kishi was in Indonesia. During his meeting with Sukarno, Kishi "suddenly abandoned our existing plan and agreed in principle to the plan [proposed by Sukarno] of cancelling the trade obligations," which "caused the tides to turn...at that point the longstanding issue of reparations was resolved at once."[2]

Apart from the reparations, Japan had proposed swapping Indonesia's trade debts with long-term loans, but Sukarno requested that the amount of the trade debt be deducted from the US$400 million reparation payment. When a Japanese diplomat present protested that Sukarno's proposal would require Japan to shoulder the interest on the long-term loan, Kishi dismissed the objection, saying: "We should not take issue with such a trivial point." In Kishi's own words, the agreement was "a decision I made in my responsibility as prime minister, with no prior approval whatsoever from the Japanese side." Sukarno, as if to offer reassurance that he could be trusted, replied, "From the war years and through the postwar years up to the present, I have always been a close friend of Japan." To this, Kishi said, "I have visited every country in Southeast Asia, and there is no other country of greater importance than yours." The Japanese side described the atmosphere of the meeting as "that of two leaders speaking heart to heart, vowing to collaborate closely in the future."[3]

What drove Kishi to conclude the negotiations? It was around this time that Japan's rapid economic growth actually began, and there was growing pressure from within the country to find overseas markets. The unresolved issue of reparations had long been a barrier to the markets in Southeast Asia. After the conclusion of negotiations with Burma and the Philippines, expectations ran high that an agreement would also be reached with Indonesia.

Meanwhile, on the political front, Japan had attained its long-sought goal of becoming a member of the United Nations in 1956. Upon its election as a non-permanent member of the Security Council in October of the following year, it began to engage in active diplomacy as if to make up for its long absence, forcefully calling for a ban on nuclear tests and presenting its own mediation plan for the Lebanon crisis of 1958. In order to expand its "diplomatic space" even further, it had become increasingly important for Japan to achieve a breakthrough in its relationship with Southeast Asia.

Kishi also had his eye on the upcoming negotiations for revising the Japan–US Security Treaty, which was at the top of his administration's agenda; through his visits to Southeast Asia, Kishi said, he sought to "fortify Japan's standing in Asia; in other words, highlighting the fact that Japan is at the center of Asia would strengthen my position when I meet Ike to negotiate a more equal relationship between Japan and the United States."[4]

For Japan, Indonesia merited the greatest attention in the region. Within the single region of Southeast Asia, there were strongholds carved out by the United States in the Philippines and by the United Kingdom in Malaya, while Thailand maintained its staunch tradition of independence. Vietnam and the other countries in Indochina were caught up in war and turmoil. Against this backdrop, Indonesia not only possessed petroleum resources and major market potential, but was also striving to shed the influence of its former Dutch rulers under the banner of anti-colonialism. Looking across Southeast Asia in search of a destination, Japan felt drawn to the promising vacuum of Indonesia.

Given Japan's interest in Indonesia as a new land that would provide it with a market and resources, as well as the extraordinary bond that developed between the two countries, some have called Indonesia the "second Manchukuo" for postwar Japan. And it is true that some individuals who had been successful in prewar Manchuria, such as Kishi himself and Yoshisuke Ayukawa, were prominent among the politicians and businessmen who took a keen interest in Indonesia.

Prior to Kishi's visit, Ataru Kobayashi was chosen from the business community as a special envoy and was dispatched to meet Sukarno. Kobayashi began by explaining how he and Kishi agreed that "Japan should not pursue an all-encompassing policy for Southeast Asia, but concentrate instead on two or three countries, particularly on Indonesia, which is closely related to Japan in terms of its geography and race." He went on to say,

> In Japan there is an ancient tradition in which we would sip each other's blood when taking an oath of brotherhood...Give us your support, so that Prime Minister Kishi and President Sukarno can sip each other's blood and form a union of brotherhood between Japan and Indonesia.[5]

Beyond "Pro-" or "Anti-" Communism

Yet, no matter how important it was to Japan, Indonesia was in the midst of a civil war. Moreover, America was busily pursuing its covert intervention in support of the insurgency. What was the thinking that led Kishi and the Japanese side to decide to conclude the reparation talks, which would indicate their commitment to Sukarno?

The Japanese Foreign Ministry's basic analysis of the situation was that the insurgents had established the revolutionary government solely as a means to force the central government into accepting their demands and that it was not likely to develop into a de facto central government. This was based on the ministry's sense that, though most Indonesians might sympathize with the demands for decentralization, they "saw the establishment of the revolutionary government as disrupting Indonesia, and saw the support given to the insurgent government by foreign countries...as a manifestation of foreign colonialism, and thus showed no support for the insurgent government." Furthermore, the ministry felt the Indonesian public placed a far higher priority on maintaining a unified nation and eliminating colonialism than on ideological issues of pro- or anti-Communism.

Based on this assessment, the Kishi administration continued to favor Sukarno throughout the civil war. During a parliamentary session, Foreign Minister Fujiyama responded to a question about whether the United States and the Netherlands would intentionally seek to weaken Indonesia to secure their oil rights. He acknowledged the possibility of such efforts in the future, and clearly stated Japan's intention to support Indonesia through reparations and economic aid so that the government would stand on a solid foundation: "We will neither enjoy nor welcome any weakening in the Indonesian government. On the contrary, we will firmly seek to nurture the central government of Indonesia so that it can develop into a respectable nation."[6]

Fujiyama's response was interpreted by the foreign media as a signal that even if America came out in support of the insurgents, Japan would support the current government as a matter of course. The comment created a stir in various countries as a challenge against the United States; the Indonesian government expressed its "deep gratitude for the spiritual support shown by Japan, and especially to comments made by Foreign Minister Fujiyama."

At the request of the Indonesian government, Prime Minister Kishi also issued a statement declaring that the situation in Indonesia was "a domestic political issue in which foreign intervention had no place." Kishi was of the opinion that before being either for or against Communism, Sukarno was above all a nationalist. The outcome of the civil war would, he felt, be decided not by the Cold War ideology of anti- or pro-Communism, but by a robust sense of nationalism with a desire for independence that viewed outside intervention as a return of colonialism. This was the underlying understanding shared by the Japanese side.

Seen from another angle, it was absolutely imperative that Indonesia be united under the nationalist Sukarno for Japan to move forward. Any advance by Japan would obviously become difficult if Indonesia were to become divided over ideology, as this would invite intervention by America and other major powers outside the region and transform it into a front line of Cold War rivalries—a "second Vietnam." The principal aspects of the Japanese stance—its indifference toward Cold War ideology and emphasis on Asian nationalism, as well as its desire to advance into Asia—were largely one and the same.

Japan considered Sukarno a nationalist and gave him high marks for his leadership and felt that even the strong showing by the Indonesian Communist Party, which had so shocked the Eisenhower administration, would not erode his influence. However, as we shall see in the following chapters, Sukarno gradually gravitated to the left, forcing Japan to make a considerable effort to restrain him in order to reduce Indonesia's association with the ideological conflict of the Cold War.

Japan to replace the Netherlands

Meanwhile, what were the motives on the Indonesian side? Even as it was undergoing the reparations talks with Japan, the start of a civil war, and American intervention, Indonesia was in the midst of another major movement. This was the confiscation of Dutch assets in Indonesia and the expulsion of Dutch nationals, which marked the final stage of Indonesia's decolonization.

While its war of independence had ended in 1949, Indonesia was forced to offer concessions that reflected the power balance at the time, such as participating in a confederation with the Netherlands and fully guaranteeing Dutch economic interests in Indonesia. As a consequence, industries that were central to the Indonesian economy—including plantation farming, financial services, and trade—remained in the hands of Dutch capital. Should it realize its independence by confiscating these businesses, or should it focus on rebuilding its devastated economy by allowing Dutch enterprises to continue their operations? The Indonesian government had been seeking to manage the country's economy through trial and error.

But there was public discontent over an economic system dominated by the Dutch, as if independence had never occurred; public sentiment against colonialism was further aroused when the Dutch refused to hand over the sovereignty of West Irian, the western region of the island of New Guinea that remained under its control. This prompted the Indonesian government to finally set course toward "Indonesianizing" its economy by renouncing its union with the Netherlands and the agreement that had guaranteed special economic rights for the Dutch.

Meanwhile, despite the five-year economic plan launched by the government in 1956 to reconstruct the Indonesian economy, the country's foreign currency reserves had become depleted by half due to the prolonged economic slump, and reparations payments from Japan represented a valuable opportunity to obtain much-needed foreign currency. As Indonesia embarked on a full-scale effort to develop its economy on its own, Japan began to demonstrate a greater presence, as its own economy recovered over the decade following the end of World War II. By 1957, Indonesia began to show an active interest in the reparations negotiations, as evidenced by a personal letter sent by Prime Minister Djuanda Kartawidjaja to Kishi.

As described previously, the reparations negotiations were concluded during Kishi's visit in November 1957, at a time when Indonesia was in the midst of a popular movement aimed at driving out the Dutch. A joint Afro-Asian resolution seeking settlement of the West Irian dispute had been presented to the UN General Assembly, and its rejection triggered large-scale strikes at Dutch-controlled companies throughout Indonesia, which resulted in them being taken over by the workers.

The Indonesian government endorsed these developments and, in December, adopted a series of hard-line policies against the Netherlands, including the closure of Dutch consulates in each region and the seizure of the Dutch flag carrier KPM, which was the main shipping company that connected the islands of Indonesia. With this move, many Dutch capital assets at the center of Indonesian economy were finally confiscated.

However, these measures had an immediate negative impact on Indonesia's economic management. With KPM's confiscation, the shipping industry was particularly hard-hit. Seeing what was coming, most ships had fled, and this left the Indonesian islands with no shipping lines between them—effectively severing the lifeline of an archipelago nation. This instantly disrupted the distribution of goods, and the price of rice doubled within a week.

Reparations talks with Japan had only just been concluded, and faced with this predicament, the Indonesian government lost no time in asking Japan to procure ships using the reparations. Negotiations were initially conducted on a private basis out of the Japanese government's consideration for the Dutch, but in the end as much as 25 percent of the total reparations were spent on shipping, including fifty-one vessels. (Incidentally, much of the questionable dealings associated with the reparations were related to shipping.)

In the matter of these ships it was particularly clear, but in other aspects as well, the Japanese advance that began with the reparations was to take on the nature of replacing the Dutch. Sukarno is reported to have asked Kishi whether Japan would step into Indonesia once the Dutch were driven out. Seen from the standpoint of Indonesia, which hoped to avoid becoming caught up in the Cold War as it sought to decolonize and achieve independence, the Japanese advance that began with its reparations was both extraordinary and significant, since it offered an alternative that carried less political risk than receiving aid from either the United States or the Soviet Union, which could have had direct implications for the Cold War.

Then again, Indonesia had been oppressively occupied by Japan in the not-so-distant past. Was there no antagonism toward Japan in connection with World War II? In reality, the Indonesian view of Japan was by no means monolithic. Among Indonesia's nationalist leaders, influential figures who had studied in the Netherlands and had learned Western values, such as the country's first vice president, Mohammad Hatta, or its first prime minister, Sutan Sjahrir, had viewed the war as a contest between democracy and fascism and considered Japanese fascism to be the primary enemy.

In contrast, Sukarno was a nationalist who had spent his formative years in Java without ever leaving his country; at times he quipped about Hatta and Sjahrir, saying more than half of their insides were European. After all, for someone like Sukarno, World War II was a war between the major powers fighting over their interests, in which Asia should not have become involved. Even during the war, it was absolutely clear to him that the Dutch colonial master was the true enemy. Japan—which would eventually overrun Indonesia—was surely an enemy, but a useful one that would benefit the cause of Indonesian independence by defeating the Dutch; collaboration with Japan could be reasoned away as a strategy.

During the three and a half years of Japanese rule, Sukarno cooperated with the military government while developing his nationalist movement, establishing himself as the unrivaled leader of the independence movement by the end of the war. Following the conclusion of reparations talks, Indonesia sought to rapidly deepen its relationship with Japan. This path was inseparably linked to the fact that power had fallen into the hands of Sukarno, whose connections to Japan were strong. Speaking often about his relationship with Japan as being "tried and true," Sukarno may have decided to use that leverage again as he aspired to eliminate the persistent vestiges of Dutch influence and accomplish "complete independence" under his leadership.

The American dilemma

As we have already seen, America envisioned the development of economic ties between Japan and Southeast Asia as a counterweight to the Communist camp and was hoping for a resolution in the reparations talks as a prerequisite. At the same time, the United States had cautiously avoided involving itself in those negotiations. Memories of the war were still vivid in people's minds, and if the United States became overtly involved, lingering resentment for Japan's wartime deeds could easily be redirected at America as well.

It was ironic that Japan's reparations negotiations with Indonesia, the keystone of Southeast Asia, had been reached in the midst of an American intervention aimed at toppling Sukarno. How did the United States view this development?

America, while providing support to the insurgency in Indonesia's civil war, was actually concerned with another grave issue: which force would fill the vacuum created in Indonesia after Sukarno eliminated the Dutch? The most disturbing outcome would be the advance of the Soviet Union and East European countries, which had offered to provide ships and engineers. The pressing issue was restoring the lifeline of the archipelago nation by providing Indonesia with ships to replace those withdrawn by the Dutch.

These were delicate circumstances, and vying to make its advance into the Indonesian vacuum—spearheaded by the reparations it had just agreed to pay—Japan launched an offensive to gain US approval.

In late December 1957, Foreign Minister Fujiyama met US Ambassador Douglas MacArthur II and, after inquiring about the US view of the Indonesian situation, warned MacArthur that economic upheaval could drive Indonesia into the arms of the Communists. Reading Fujiyama's intentions, MacArthur sought to apply the brakes on any blatant action by the Japanese. He recounted telling Fujiyama:

> [the] present situation was indeed disturbing. I said I recognized long-term importance of Indonesia to Japan, particularly in economic and trade fields, but I thought that it was important that Japan not take actions which could be interpreted as helping to dislodge [the] Dutch.[7]

Three days later, Fujiyama explained to MacArthur that the Indonesian government was preparing to charter ships owned by Japanese companies to replace the Dutch ships that had been withdrawn. He added that Indonesia must be prevented from turning to the Communist bloc over an issue such as the procurement of ships. Fujiyama also explained how he himself would travel to Jakarta next month to formally sign the reparations agreement.

Not knowing how to respond, MacArthur sought instructions from the State Department. Meanwhile, in Washington, top leaders of the Eisenhower administration were faced with a dilemma: on the one hand, it was becoming increasingly uncertain whether US intervention in the Indonesian civil war would succeed, while on the other, there was a mounting sense of crisis that the Indonesian vacuum would be filled by the Communists.

A few days later, MacArthur explained his government's position to Fujiyama, saying that while the United States did not approve of Indonesia's hard-line measures against the Netherlands, it was nevertheless concerned about the Communist side filling the vacuum in Indonesia. Fujiyama responded by repeatedly stressing Japan's willingness to "play a constructive role in preventing the Communists from filling the Indonesian void." America may have resented Japan's claim to the noble cause of "anti-Communism" when it was actually maneuvering to replace the Dutch, but then again, it had no choice but to approve.

While Japan and America were engaged in these discussions, the situation in Indonesia took a sudden turn in March 1958. Against the expectations of most observers both inside and outside the country, the central government in Jakarta launched a military campaign to quell the insurgency. Once fighting broke out, the armed resistance by the insurgents, whose main demand had been nothing more than decentralization of authority, proved fragile. Bukittinggi, the designated capital of the revolutionary government, fell in less than two months. In May, a fighter aircraft that had been assisting the insurgents was shot down, and with the capture of its American pilot, the CIA's covert operations came to light. And in the course of these events, Sukarno saw a considerable rise in his influence at home.

Forced into a corner, the US government had no choice but to reverse its policy, and by the end of May, Secretary of State Dulles commented that "the situation in Indonesia is an issue that should be resolved by Indonesia." To begin with, the CIA had played a central role in the round of US interventions in the Indonesian civil war—not only in terms of their execution, but starting with the initial intelligence analysis, leaving the State Department and the local US Embassy in the dark.

Furthermore, as if acting in advance to gratify the Dulles brothers (John Foster Dulles, the elder, was Secretary of State; the younger, Alan, was head of the CIA)—who both emphasized countering Communism and were enthusiastic about intervening in Indonesia—the CIA had continued to dispatch biased intelligence that gave the impression that American intervention would quickly lead to the creation of an anti-Communist Indonesia.

Not only did the US intervention end in failure as a consequence, but it had the exact opposite effect of considerably strengthening Sukarno's position, in what was described as "one of the most misguided, ill-conceived, and ultimately counterproductive covert operations of the entire Cold War era."[8]

In a parallel development, America changed its attitude toward Japan's advance into Indonesia. In mid-May, Ambassador MacArthur told the Japanese side that with the issue of reparations resolved, Indonesia's affinity toward Japan placed them in the best position to encourage a settlement between the central government in Jakarta and the insurgency.

MacArthur also urged Japan to persuade Sukarno that it would be better to compromise, since the insurgency was not expected to be easily defeated. He also asked Japan to offer Indonesia the use of Japanese seamen as an alternative to the Soviet offer of ships and crewmen and to provide consumer goods requested by Indonesia that were currently being supplied by the Soviet Union.

Having failed in its attempt at intervention, achieving a soft landing for the civil war in Indonesia and preventing the spread of Soviet influence were now pressing issues for America. Since it was directly involved in the civil war, however, any attempt made by the United States on either issue was sure to draw fire from the Indonesian side. Japan, on the other hand, had successfully reentered Indonesia by means of reparations, thereby keeping its distance from the Cold War, and also belonged to the group of Asian-African countries. As America struggled to cope with the rising tide of Asian nationalism, it began to see Japan as a perfect stand-in.

Reparations and "the return to Asia"

As we have seen, Japan's reparations to Indonesia were settled amid the interplay of varied political dynamics and national motives. Due in part to the delayed establishment of an Indonesian institution that was to oversee the implementation of reparations, however, it was not until 1959 that an agreement was reached on an implementation plan for the first year of payments.

Most of the reparations were spent on ships, river development, and construction of paper and textile factories, hotels, and department stores. However, there were a number of shady deals that were questioned by the Japanese parliament. In one case, a used ship was delivered to the Indonesian side in the name of reparations at three times the market price, with the difference suspected to have been rechanneled as political funding. Moreover, not many of the factories and facilities built under the reparations program operated consistently in later years. Japan has admitted more or less publicly that there were problems on its side as well, raising doubts about whether the reparations contributed to any real development in the Indonesian economy.

On the other hand, since they took the form of provision of services, a significant portion of the reparations were returned to Japan through the Japanese companies that received the orders. The reparations also presented these companies with a golden opportunity to penetrate deeply into the Indonesian market by implementing the contracts. As we will see in the following chapters, due to the economic constraints that accompanied Sukarno's shift to the left, Indonesia would effectively use up the reparations it received from Japan by 1965. Yet, even in the years that followed, Indonesia continued to be the top recipient of Japan's foreign aid and remained one of the leading destinations for Japanese investment among developing countries. The reparations allowed Japan to develop an intimate relationship with Indonesia that went far beyond the original purpose of atoning for damages it had inflicted during the war.

Japan slipped into the vacuum created by decolonization with tacit approval from the United States, which was concerned about the spreading influence of the Communist bloc. Japan's southward advance became a reality as the two major tides in postwar Asia—decolonization and the Cold War—overlapped.

At the same time, the bond forged between Kishi and Sukarno by "sipping each other's blood in a vow of brotherhood" may have been evidence of a certain sense of Pan-Asianism that was unrelated to the Cold War. It is true that those on the Japanese side seized every opportunity to present the Indonesian side with the argument that Japan, with its technological prowess, and Indonesia, with its bountiful resources, made a complementary pair and that collaboration between the two countries would lead not only to mutual prosperity but contribute significantly to the development of Asia as a whole. But this was in fact the very same rhetoric that had repeatedly been used throughout the war during the era of the Greater East Asia Co-Prosperity Sphere.

If Japan were to align itself with the United States and face Asia along Cold War lines, Indonesia under Sukarno could be lost to the other side of the Cold War wall as an opponent to be confronted. In fact, pro-Western countries such as South Korea and Taiwan, along with the United Kingdom and Australia, did cooperate either directly or indirectly with the US intervention in the Indonesian civil war, the goal of which was to topple Sukarno and dismantle Indonesia.

Conversely, if Japan were to recognize Sukarno as a nationalist, as Kishi had repeatedly insisted, the decolonization policy pursued by Sukarno could signify the emergence of a new land for Japan—which was presenting itself as a member of Asia, and open up a vast expanse of Asia ahead. By distancing itself from the Cold War ideology, Japan could expand the scope of its "return to Asia." Here, we can see a common theme that runs through such thinking and the path chosen by Japan at the Bandung Conference. There was an underlying awareness among the Japanese that, once the Western colonies in Southeast Asia were driven out, a new land would emerge for Japan to move into. Perhaps this was evidence of Japan's consistent impulse to pursue a southward advance, which had existed before World War II and remained unchanged since.

However, as Sukarno subsequently took up the cause of accomplishing a revolutionary independence and began to lean increasingly toward the left, Japan's southward advance was to become a growing dilemma. And in the course of these developments, Japan became embroiled in a feud with the United Kingdom, which continued to maintain the vestiges of an empire in the region from its base in Singapore, and in a tug-of-war over Indonesia with Communist China, which was the general headquarters of revolution in postwar Asia.

Notes

1 Hiroshi Yashiki, "Baisho to keizai kyoryoku" [Reparations and Economic Aid], *Tsusho sangyo kenkyu* 5 [International Trade and Industry Studies 5], no. 6 (June 1957): 57.
2 "Regarding Japan-Indonesia negotiations," dispatch from Minister Takagi to Minister of Foreign Affairs Fujiyama, November 29, 1957, Diplomatic Record of the Ministry of Foreign Affairs of Japan, B'0152.
3 "First meeting between Prime Minister Kishi and President Sukarno," November 27, 1957, Diplomatic Record of the Ministry of Foreign Affairs of Japan, B'0152.
4 Nobusuke Kishi, *Kishi Nobusuke kaikoroku* [Memoirs of Nobusuke Kishi] (Tokyo: Kosaido Publishing, 1983), 312.
5 "Meeting between Special Ambassador Kobayashi and President Sukarno," September 23, 1957, Diplomatic Record of the Ministry of Foreign Affairs of Japan, B'0152. "Background of reparations negotiations with Indonesia" Report, Asian Affairs Bureau Third Division, March 1958, Diplomatic Record of the Ministry of Foreign Affairs of Japan, B'0152.
6 March 1958, Lower House Foreign Affairs Committee.
7 "Tokyo to Department of State, December 24, 1957," *FRUS, 1955–1957*, vol. 22.
8 Robert J. McMahon, *The Limits of Empire: The United States and Southeast Asia since World War II* (New York: Columbia University Press, 1999), 88.

3 Seeking to influence the course of decolonization

Japan's rivalry with the United Kingdom, tug-of-war with China

Figure 3.1 From right: LDP Vice President Shojiro Kawashima, Indonesia's President Sukarno, and China's Premier Zhou Enlai, upon the tenth anniversary of the Bandung Conference; April 19, 1965, Jakarta.

Source: © AP/AFLO.

Deepening of the "southward advance" and its outcome

In its "southward advance" that began with wartime reparations, postwar Japan found itself moving ever deeper into Indonesia, the anchor of maritime Asia. This was inextricably linked to the fact that Indonesia under Sukarno, the region's leading nationalist, was most forceful in seeking the goal of achieving complete independence and promoting decolonization. Postwar Japan had been thwarted by the walls of the Cold War in Northeast Asia, and so its energy was redirected southward, as if drawn by the tide of decolonization.

Speaking of decolonization, we should recall that imperial Japan had itself been a colonial empire that effectively ruled over Korea, Taiwan, and Manchukuo until defeat in war caused its demise. So there was a certain irony in postwar Japan's "southward advance," which could also be interpreted as a phenomenon in which Japan, having lost its colonies in Northeast Asia through its defeat, moved into the vacuum left by Western colonizers once they were ousted from Southeast Asia.

Japan's own colonies had automatically been dismantled following its defeat and were quickly transformed into staging areas for ideological conflict, such as the civil war between the Nationalists and Communists in China and the Korean War. Consequently, Japan came to view developments in Northeast Asia primarily in the context of the Cold War. Setting aside the question of whether this was good or bad, Japan had thus lost an opportunity to come face to face with decolonization as an issue of direct concern to itself. And as it proceeded with its "southward advance" into Southeast Asia, postwar Japan began to see the issue of decolonization with sympathy for Asian nationalism and its aspirations for independence, while it also saw a potential opportunity as the departure of former colonial masters of the West cleared the way for its advance.

But the outcome of decolonization was highly unpredictable. As evidenced by the US effort to overthrow Sukarno—who was suspected of leaning toward Communism—the drive toward decolonization inevitably touched on the Cold War issue of which side the newly independent countries would choose: the Eastern bloc or the Western bloc. Likewise, Japan could not pursue its "southward advance" further without raising tensions between itself and the United Kingdom, as well as other former colonial powers that still remained in Southeast Asia.

While there were other countries that Japan was drawn to, such as Burma, it was Sukarno's Indonesia that ultimately figured overwhelmingly in Japan's "southward advance." But Sukarno himself remained obsessed with accomplishing independence. Once he had expelled Dutch capital from Indonesia and dealt with the unfinished business of retaking West Irian from the Netherlands, Sukarno turned to his next target, triggering a dispute over Malaysia with the United Kingdom, which continued to maintain a major presence in maritime Asia. Further, as Sukarno grew increasingly radical in his ideology, he began to rapidly gravitate toward Communist China.

Japan had cast its lot with Sukarno, and as the British Empire began to unravel in Southeast Asia and as China in its radicalization headed toward the Cultural Revolution, Japan's "southward advance" became mired in difficulties and dilemmas. The clash between countries that converged in Sukarno's Indonesia was a battle, fought without weapons, over the outcome of decolonization and the future of Asian order.

Attempts at rebuilding the British Empire

When we look at Southeast Asia past and present, one of the most prominent differences is the presence and absence of the United Kingdom. In the heyday of the British Empire, the line stretching from the British homeland through the Suez Canal and India and on to Australia and New Zealand formed the backbone of the empire, and Singapore was its stronghold in Southeast Asia. While France and the Netherlands were ousted from their former colonies in Southeast Asia after World War II, the United Kingdom remained a major power in maritime Asia and continued to control Singapore and Malaya, as well as Sabah and Sarawak in North Borneo.

But even the British were finding it difficult to stem the rising global tide of decolonization and nationalism. If Britain persisted in keeping its colonies even as the French and Dutch fled Southeast Asia, it risked becoming a perfect target of Asian nationalism. Moreover, having been ravaged by two world wars, the country could not bear the financial burden of maintaining and defending its colonies.

Under these circumstances, the British chose the path of granting independence to its colonies in Southeast Asia while keeping them on a tight leash within an "unofficial empire." Britain gave Malaya its independence in 1957 and sought to realign Singapore, Sabah, and Sarawak by incorporating them into Malaya in the early 1960s. This was the archetype that led to the formation of today's Malaysia (Singapore subsequently separated from this union).

However, Sukarno vehemently protested the plan, which he saw as a "neo-colonialist conspiracy to lay siege to Indonesia," and the situation developed into the Indonesia–Malaysia confrontation that roiled maritime Southeast Asia in the early 1960s.

Let us first examine the British plan for Malaysia. The British thought the key to retaining influence over its unofficial empire in Southeast Asia lay in ensuring the stability of Singapore, which was its major military base. Struggling with the situation in Vietnam, the United States was eager to have the British retain a military presence in the region; it was also important for the United Kingdom itself in maintaining its influence over Australia and New Zealand. It was thought that "without Singapore, British influence in the region will deteriorate to a level comparable to that of France."[1]

Yet in reality, Singapore was unstable. Leftist groups were spreading their influence among the Chinese workers that constituted the majority of the population, appealing to their sense of belonging to mainland China to gain support for Communism. If these groups were to seize power from Prime Minister Lee Kuan Yew and the small number of pro-British elites, it seemed imminently possible that Singapore would quickly become a "Cuba of the eastern hemisphere" ruled by a leftist regime.

To prevent such a situation, the British considered incorporating Singapore into the Federation of Malaya, which was clearly anti-Communist. The problem was that Malaya rested on a precarious balance between the ethnic Malays, who comprised 50 percent of the population, and the ethnic Chinese, who accounted for a little over 40 percent. If Singapore—where ethnic Chinese figured significantly—were brought into this mix, ethnic Malays would be outnumbered by ethnic Chinese in the new nation. As a solution, regions in North Borneo such as Sabah and Sarawak were also to be included in the merger, so as to maintain a population balance in which ethnic Malays retained the majority. This plan for Malaysia was made public by Tunku Abdul Rahman, prime minister of the Federation of Malaya, in May 1961.

Neighboring Indonesia offered no public reaction at the time, since its conflict with the Dutch over the jurisdiction of West Irian had entered a critical stage. It later reversed its attitude, however, when a leftist revolt broke out in Brunei, a region of North Borneo that was being considered for incorporation into Malaysia. Indonesia began accusing Britain of forcibly implementing the Malaysia plan and suppressing the will of the people expressed through the rebellion. Over time, it stepped up its criticism to the point of seeking to destroy the plan as a neo-colonialist conspiracy aimed at encircling Indonesia.

Witnessing the buildup of Indonesian antagonism toward Malaysia, the British began to harbor a growing suspicion that Indonesia's motives lay not only in obstructing the creation of Malaysia, but in realizing a "Greater Indonesia" that would unite ethnic Malays. Indonesia and the Malay Peninsula were part of the same culture to begin with, and there had been groups within the independence movement during the colonial era that advocated merging the two into an independent "Greater Indonesia." The British suspected that Sukarno's true goal might lie in annexing Malaysia to create such an entity.

From Sukarno's point of view, the United States, with support from the United Kingdom and Malaya, had taken advantage of the insurgency in Indonesia that lasted from 1957 to 1958 by intervening with the aim of disrupting his regime and dismantling the country. With this crisis still fresh in his memory, the possibility of neighboring countries and extra-regional powers scheming to contain Indonesia was no fantasy for Sukarno.

Another factor at work was the perception gap between Indonesia and Malaya concerning what constituted a threat. From the late 1940s through the 1950s, Malaya had spent much time and effort on suppressing an uprising led by the Malayan Communist Party and thus considered Communism to be the greatest threat to Malaya.

In contrast, Indonesia had fought hard against colonialism, not least in its war of independence from the Netherlands, and saw colonialism as the biggest threat. It was also strongly conscious of its status as a global leader of the decolonization movement that had hosted the Bandung Conference. In Sukarno's view, an easily achieved independence that retained close ties with a former colonial ruler, like that achieved by Malaya, did not constitute true independence.

Sukarno's regime of contradictions

As we have seen, there were various factors that led to the Indonesian policy of confrontation with Malaysia, but foremost among them was the country's internal political dynamics under Sukarno, which were the politics of independence and revolution. Even after the war of independence, Sukarno stressed that independence and the accompanying revolution would not end until West Irian was restored. In the process, he would bring about a social revolution by uniting people who had nothing in common other than the fact that they had been subjected to Dutch colonial rule and transforming them into citizens of Indonesia. This was the path envisioned by Sukarno.

He was opposed by influential politicians and political parties who claimed that the revolution had run its course now that independence was achieved and it was time for nation-building. But the opposition was based in the Outer Islands and lost its influence in the civil war that began in 1957. As the Constitutional Assembly and political parties fell into disarray, Sukarno seized power by allying with the army to form a new regime in which the will of the people was to be embodied by Sukarno, who was the "extension of the people's tongues," rather than through an assembly or through elections. Sukarno secured a predominant position for himself under this system, which was called "guided democracy," and forged ahead to "liberate" West Irian.

Sukarno poured his energy into military expansion and was prepared to use force, but through the mediation of US President John F. Kennedy, West Irian was placed under Indonesian jurisdiction. This was supposed to be the consummation of Indonesia's independence. It was hoped that once the West Irian issue was concluded to its satisfaction, Indonesia would shift to a more moderate policy of emphasizing domestic economic development. That was precisely why Kennedy himself stepped in to mediate over the objections of the Dutch.

But the economic reforms introduced in collaboration with the International Monetary Fund (IMF) called for an austere fiscal policy that was unpopular with the Indonesian people. And while he had joined forces with the army to weaken the political parties in the process of seizing power, Sukarno was now actively defending the rise of Indonesia's Communist Party in order to check the growing influence of the army. As a result, he created a regime in which he held the upper hand by being the one person capable of striking a balance between the two conflicting groups. However, both the army and the Communist Party—which were now the two prominent forces in the country—preferred to see a new crisis emerge out of the confrontation with Malaysia rather than a shift to nation-building in cooperation with the IMF.

For the Communist Party, a new crisis would present a perfect opportunity to fend off the army's stranglehold and seize the initiative by appealing for a continuation of the revolution. On the other hand, any progress in the IMF-led economic reforms would lead to a deepening of Indonesia's relationship with the Western bloc countries, which was a most unwelcome prospect. A new crisis would also be convenient for the army, as it was seeking to maintain the inflated scope of its troops and budget in the wake of the

West Irian conflict. Furthermore, the army had been accused of being unco-operative by the Communist Party, which had taken a consistently aggres-sive stand during the conflict. It needed to avoid inviting similar criticism in the conflict with Malaysia.

The political dynamics of the Sukarno regime therefore made it difficult to shift from "independence and revolution" to a policy of economic reform. The alternative was to present the new cause of confronting Malaysia and defeating neo-colonialism as the next course of action following the return of West Irian to maintain the diplomatic tensions and bloated budgets. This was by far the easier political choice. It was becoming increasingly difficult for Sukarno to admit that independence had been achieved and to steer the country in a distinctly different direction—toward the major challenge of building its domestic economy.

In 1963, Indonesian Foreign Minister Subandrio issued an official warn-ing that the forced formation of Malaysia could lead to a military clash. And in another development, the conflict spilled over to the Philippines, which began claiming territorial rights over Sabah, a region in North Borneo that was part of the Malaysia plan. Sabah had originally belonged to the Sultanate of Sulu, which was subsequently annexed to the Philippines. The claim was that the Sultan of Sulu had only loaned Sabah to a British com-pany and that sovereignty therefore remained with the Philippines.

At this time, growing friction with the United States had led to a surge in nationalism in the Philippines, and President Diosdado Macapagal intended to ride this wave by taking up the territorial issue. Thus the Malaysia plan developed into an issue involving the Philippines in addition to Indonesia.

Yet the conflict did not flare up instantly. Although Foreign Minister Subandrio repeatedly criticized the plan, the meaning of "confrontation" remained vague. In an effort to bring the situation under control, ministers from Indonesia, Malaya, and the Philippines met in Manila in June, where a discussion took place on the Greater Malayan Confederation proposed by the Philippines.

The Greater Malayan Confederation was envisioned as uniting ethnic Malays in Indonesia and Malaya, as well as in the Philippines, in their common interest. Through this new proposal, President Macapagal sought to shelve the deadlocked territorial issue of Sabah while presenting a new diplomatic framework that would replace their dependence on the United States.

As a result of their consultations, Indonesia and the Philippines agreed not to object to the formation of Malaysia, provided that public opinion in North Borneo was confirmed under the auspices of the United Nations. They also agreed in principle to the formation of the Greater Malayan Confederation.

Just as it seemed the conflict would be resolved peacefully, events sud-denly took a turn in the opposite direction. The formation of the Federation of Malaysia was announced with complete disregard for the preconditions agreed upon in Manila, which included a public opinion survey in North Borneo.

Naturally, Indonesia and the Philippines were enraged. Yet, Indonesia, Malaya, and the Philippines met once again for a tripartite summit in Manila, where they reached an accord to postpone the formation of the Federation of Malaysia from the scheduled date of August 31 so that a UN commission could conduct a survey of public opinion in North Borneo. They also agreed to promote the Greater Malayan Confederation proposed by the Philippines under the name "Maphilindo."

Following this agreement, the UN commission began its survey to establish public opinion in Borneo. But before the results of the survey were known, the Malayan government announced that the Federation of Malaysia would be established on September 16. The move was met with vehement objection and protest from Indonesia and the Philippines, who wanted to know what the point of conducting a survey was if the formation of Malaysia was to be decided without waiting for the results.

Escalation of the Malaysian conflict

British intentions were at work behind the apparently provocative stance taken by Malaya. The United Kingdom was strongly opposed to intervention by Indonesia and the Philippines in affairs concerning territories under its control. Moreover, if a UN survey on public opinion were to become a prerequisite for seeking independence, it might create an unwelcome precedent for the United Kingdom, which still held numerous colonies in Africa and elsewhere. The Manila Accord was an unacceptable compromise for the British.

In addition, Malaya and Singapore, which were to be part of the Federation of Malaysia, differed in their industrial structures and were completely at odds with each other on the issues of unifying their markets and the right to levy taxes. It had taken quite an effort to contain such tensions and reach this point. And now that the formation of a new nation was imminent, the British believed that in the worst-case scenario, postponing its formation could result in the unraveling of the Malaysia plan itself.

On September 14, the UN announced the results of its survey, which showed that the people of North Borneo favored joining Malaysia. Two days later, the new nation of Malaysia was formed as planned. However, Indonesia refused to recognize Malaysia on the grounds that it had violated its commitment by deciding to form a new nation without waiting for the survey results; the Philippines also withheld recognition of the newly formed nation.

In response, the Malaysian government announced it had severed diplomatic relations with Indonesia and the Philippines, which led angry masses in Jakarta to attack the British Embassy and raze it to the ground. Meanwhile, the Indonesian government adhered to its stated policy of confrontation with Malaysia and made no move to prevent British companies from being taken over.

The international community responded harshly to Indonesia's seemingly extreme behavior, such as the burning of the British Embassy. The IMF discontinued its emergency loan, and the United States announced it was suspending additional aid. Then in November came the sudden death of Prime Minister Djuanda, who had led the economic reforms; this put an end to Indonesia's policy of collaborating with the IMF on economic reforms. In its place, Sukarno was faced with growing pressure from the army and the Communist Party, both of which were seeking a new crisis in the form of a confrontation with Malaysia based on their respective agendas. Hereafter, Sukarno began to advocate "crushing Malaysia" and stepped up military pressure through repeated infiltrations by guerrillas and "voluntary troops" dispatched from its border in Borneo.

Britain, under its military alliance with Malaysia, was obliged to respond by sending a considerable number of troops. Contrary to its original intention of alleviating the high costs of maintaining its colonies by promoting the Malaysia plan, the United Kingdom was now faced with growing tensions and a sudden rise in military expenditures. Finding itself in a tight spot, the United Kingdom requested that its commonwealth countries Australia and New Zealand send their troops to Malaysia.

If the conflict were to develop into a full-scale military confrontation, it would set in motion the ANZUS Treaty—the security agreement concluded by Australia and New Zealand with the United States—thus raising the possibility of US involvement. And indeed, the true aim of the United Kingdom was to draw the United States to its side through the ANZUS Treaty. But for America, which was already caught up in the quagmire of Vietnam, involvement in a second conflict in Southeast Asia was to be avoided at all costs.

In this way, the Malaysian dispute was rapidly transformed into an international conflict involving many countries. For Japan, which had achieved its "southward advance" on the back of its reparations payments, the situation represented an opportunity to once again assume a political role in Asia; accordingly, Prime Minister Hayato Ikeda set out to mediate the conflict.

Hayato Ikeda steps up as mediator

Following Prime Minister Kishi's resignation amid the turmoil caused by the revised Japan–US Security Treaty, Hayato Ikeda became prime minister, calling for "tolerance and endurance." It was Ikeda who pulled the country out of Kishi's intimidating push toward nationalism and shifted the focus to the economy by launching his "income-doubling" plan. The period under the Ikeda administration was also a time when Japan saw its national strength increase in line with its economic growth, as Japan sought a place for itself in the international community. In an effort to give shape to this quest, Ikeda stressed that Japan, the United States, and Europe constituted the "three pillars of the free world." Similarly, as we shall see, behind his attempt at mediation was the intention of expanding Japan's role to the political domain.

Ikeda's decision to mediate the Malaysian conflict came during preparations for his tour of Southeast Asia in September 1963; the situation suddenly escalated following incidents such as the burning of the British Embassy. The visit itself had been scheduled in advance with the aim of nurturing friendship and goodwill. But it quickly took on political overtones, since the tour would include the central players in the conflict, such as Indonesia and the Philippines. It was Ikeda himself who decided to use this as an opportunity for mediation.

"Japan, the US, and Europe as the three pillars" was Ikeda's cherished belief, but it was nothing more than a slogan at the time. For Ikeda, stepping up as mediator in the Malaysian conflict was an opportunity to demonstrate that Japan was indeed part of the "three pillars," capable of playing a unique role in Asia that could not be filled by Western countries. He was no doubt emboldened by the trips he had made beforehand to the United States and Europe, in which Western leaders requested that Japan reason with Sukarno.

Meanwhile, the expectation in Japan was that the parliament would be dissolved and general elections would take place within the year. Foremost on Ikeda's mind was to bring about a desirable course of events in which he would dissolve parliament and call for elections, emerge victorious by highlighting his accomplishment of mediating an international conflict, and go on to win a third term in the election for the Liberal Democratic Party (LDP) leadership by defeating Eisaku Sato, who was expected to declare his candidacy. In any event, Japan was a defeated country that had hitherto been preoccupied with settling its postwar scores, including reparations, in its Asian diplomacy. This was to be an initiative in a completely new domain.

However, Japan's aggressive stance toward Asia did not emerge solely out of Ikeda's political agenda; in the backdrop was Japan's burgeoning sense of confidence toward Asia at the time. Ikeda had visited Nehru's India during a trip to Asia two years ago, and his aide wrote of his impressions upon arriving at Calcutta (now called Kolkata) as follows:

> When we turned our eyes on the crowd of people who greeted us at the airport, the first thing that struck us was that most of them were barefoot. As we drove from the airport toward the center of the city, poverty was increasingly evident. One of the main purposes of this goodwill visit was the meeting between Ikeda and Nehru, a renowned international statesman. But having witnessed India's poverty, a sense of Japanese pride and confidence filled the hearts of Ikeda and the accompanying reporters alike. And this became the underlying spirit that stayed with us throughout our Southeast Asian visit.[2]

There was a time when Nehru displayed great brilliance as the leader of Asian non-alignment at the Bandung Conference. But over the years, the border dispute with China had deepened his antagonism toward the country, which had once been a fellow champion of the Five Principles of Peaceful Coexistence. In the end, a major military conflict between India and China broke out in 1962. The Indian army took flight, leaving the border region in a state of panic. In another area, Nehru had sought to incorporate elements of socialism into his economic policies, yet the results were far from successful. In 1964, Nehru died amid disappointment.

The aforementioned aide concluded his account of Ikeda's historic visit to Asia with the following words:

> While modern buildings line the main streets of their major cities, behind them the extreme poverty of Asian lives was laid bare. I sensed that in their pursuit of affluence, these people were about to choose either the Chinese Communist way or the Japanese way. Ikeda, too, must have felt the same. He must have also gained a piercing awareness of the indescribably important role Japan must play in Asia. We understood that the path taken by the Japanese people would become a benchmark for the people of Asia in choosing their path for the future.[3]

This was no longer the Asia that had rallied under a unified desire for independence at the Bandung Conference. For Japan, which had struggled to find its place in Bandung at the time, witnessing Asia in the grip of confusion gave it a sense of assurance regarding the significance of its role in deciding the future of Asia.

America hits the brakes

On September 23, 1963, Ikeda and his entourage left Japan for the first stop, the Philippines. What specific mediation plan did Ikeda have in mind? He revealed to US Ambassador Edwin O. Reischauer, whom he visited prior to his departure, that he intended to gather representatives from Japan, Indonesia, the Philippines, Australia, and New Zealand in Tokyo the following year to begin talks on the formation of a "West Pacific Organization." The aim was to guide the conflict to a solution by drawing Indonesia closer to the free-world countries of the Asia-Pacific.

Though Reischauer had his doubts about the feasibility of the plan, he appreciated the fact that Japan had taken the initiative of coming up with a positive proposal and advised Washington to at least show moral support. This was in line with the Kennedy administration's policy of expecting Japan to play a greater role in Asian issues.

Yet, the US State Department responded by asking Reischauer to block Ikeda's plan because it was inappropriate. In seeking a solution to the Malaysian dispute, the State Department was hanging its hopes on the

Maphilindo plan led by the Philippines and thought there was a strong like-lihood that Sukarno would use Ikeda's proposal as an excuse to sidestep the Maphilindo plan.

But Ikeda had already left Japan. As he himself admitted to the news-papers at the time, there was clearly an unrehearsed element to the pro-posal, which lacked prior consultation. Once he arrived in the Philippines, Ikeda lost no time in laying out his plan during his meeting with President Macapagal, who firmly refrained from discussing the details, saying only that although such a plan was "ultimately desirable," it would require sufficient prior understanding. Ikeda's plan had hit a wall from the onset.

Macapagal was the leader of the Maphilindo plan advocating the forma-tion of a federation of ethnic Malay countries, to which the United States had also given its support. He was not about to let Ikeda take the initiative of forming a regional plan for Asia away from him. In addition, anti-Japanese sentiment was strong in the Philippines, which had suffered tremendously during the war, and accepting Ikeda's mediation could become a domestic political issue if it were perceived as a move that acknowledged Japan's lead-ership in Asia.

Faced with the negative reaction from the Filipino side, Japan sought to deny the very fact that Ikeda had made such a proposal. But the local papers were quick to report the news, and Japan had to scramble to dismiss the reports.

At his next stop, in Indonesia, Ikeda was greeted by Prime Minister Djuanda and Madame Dewi, Sukarno's Japan-born third wife. While Sukarno welcomed Ikeda's proposal, Ikeda clearly stated that his prior-ity was "to create an atmosphere in which a tripartite meeting [between Indonesia, Malaysia, and the Philippines] could take place before I set off for the five-country summit meeting," but made it clear that he was not pre-pared to mediate at that point.[4] Ikeda was seeking to modify his course in line with US demands.

At the same time, he stressed that Japan and Indonesia were "brothers" and told Sukarno, "If there are issues the Indonesian government found difficult to bring up directly with the governments of the United States or the United Kingdom, I would gladly act as a messenger."[5] Japan adopted a stance of active engagement, agreeing to additional loans and preconditions for business expansion by Japanese companies, which was made even more conspicuous in contrast to the decisions made by Western countries and the IMF to suspend economic aid to Indonesia for the time being.

Japan, too, was certainly aware of the instability of Sukarno's regime, which was being sustained by his balancing act between the army and the Commu-nist Party. Yet Sukarno was firmly in control of the army, and above all, there was no one else who could take his place, which led Japan to conclude that "it would be safe to assume that his administration will be maintained."[6]

During his stay in Jakarta, Ikeda also met individually with the American and British ambassadors to Indonesia. Ikeda told US Ambassador Howard

Jones that "Japan and the US must save Indonesia under the IMF umbrella" and advocated a policy of engagement. In response, Jones explained that while the United States had put a freeze on new aid to Indonesia, its existing aid was being maintained.

For the Kennedy administration, Sukarno was a troublesome figure who was destabilizing the region. But in the absence of any domestic group that could challenge him, the United States could not take a hard-line stance and risk sending Indonesia into the arms of the Chinese and the Soviets. The US government policy at the time was to wait for an improvement in the situation by avoiding any moves that could make it difficult to repair its relationship with Sukarno while demonstrating some measure of sternness in view of its relationship with Congress and the United Kingdom, which were becoming increasingly antagonistic toward Sukarno. While this was not as aggressive as the "policy of engagement" advocated by Japan, there was a shared understanding between Japan and the United States regarding the importance of keeping Sukarno on their side.

The gap between the United States and United Kingdom

During his meeting with British Ambassador Andrew Gilchrist, Ikeda said that promoting the Maphilindo plan was the best course for resolving the conflict and expressed his hope that the United Kingdom would not prevent Malaysia from approving the plan. The Japanese side was evidently concerned about British interference.

As opposed to the Americans, who were counting on the Maphilindo plan as a solution to the conflict, the British saw it as a ploy to tear Malaysia away from their influence and ultimately eliminate the United Kingdom from Southeast Asia. The underlying reason for this disparity lay in the conflicting regional interests of the United States and United Kingdom.

The British thought it was most important to resolutely face Sukarno and not concede any points. In the meantime, as the Indonesian economy sank into deeper disarray, the Indonesian army could be counted upon to step in and topple Sukarno in a coup d'état. The army was no different from Sukarno in its desire for a confrontation with Malaysia, but the British had concluded that having the army in power was preferable to either the continuation of the Sukarno regime or the rise of a Communist government.

Meanwhile, the United States believed Sukarno's regime was not as vulnerable as the British thought. In its view, taking a hard-line attitude toward Sukarno was more likely to result in expanding the influence of China and the Indonesian Communist Party in Indonesia and even to an escalation in the confrontation with Malaysia. Even if Sukarno could be defeated, power could fall into the hands of the Communists. In any event, from the US point of view, the hard-line policy taken by the British would create chaos in the largest country in the region.

In other words, the gap between the United States and the United Kingdom could be explained as follows: The United States considered Indonesia important for its strategic significance and national scale as a country that could affect the global power balance and took this as the starting point when deciding its own approach and policy. For the United Kingdom, however, the overarching imperative was to ensure that the decolonization of Malaysia proceeded as planned so it could maintain an unofficial empire; Sukarno's Indonesia presented the biggest obstacle to this objective.

The British were concerned that when push came to shove, the Americans—with their emphasis on Indonesia—might opt to sacrifice Malaysia. To prevent this scenario, Britain asked Australia and New Zealand to send their troops, so as to draw the United States—which had signed the ANZUS Treaty with those two countries—to its side.

Japan was calling on the United States to adopt a policy of engagement toward Sukarno and was even more supportive of Indonesia than America was. Ikeda was advocating Japan–US–UK cooperation on Indonesia, but in reality it was a tug-of-war between the United Kingdom—protector of Malaysia and adversary of Sukarno—on one side, and Japan—which was seeking to accelerate the pace of its "southward advance" by supporting Sukarno—on the other, with each trying to draw the United States into its camp. At this point, there was a considerable gap between Japan, which emphasized engaging Sukarno, and the United Kingdom, which sought to contain Sukarno.

By containing the Sukarno regime, Britain was aiming to bring about its downfall, or at least to get it to abandon its confrontation with Malaysia. In view of this goal, the continuous aid being provided by other free-world countries such as the United States was simply spoiling British efforts.

Japan's behavior, based on its declared support for Sukarno, was particularly unacceptable. For example, when Japan exported tankers to Indonesia, the United Kingdom filed an objection with the Japanese government, on the grounds that Indonesia's current difficulty in procuring vessels is the result of the United Kingdom's ongoing economic blockade of Indonesia and that it was deplorable that Indonesia was strengthening its resistance to this policy due to vessels provided by Japan under generous conditions.[7]

In response, the Japanese side took the stance that as Indonesia's neighbor, maintaining regional stability was of vital interest to Japan, thus flatly rejecting the hard-line policy taken by the United Kingdom.

The extent of British irritation with Japan's attitude is evident in a public dispatch from the British Foreign Office, which noted that while Japan remains convinced that an excessively harsh policy against Indonesia would have an adverse effect, the true difficulty for the British lay in the Japanese view that the United Kingdom and United States are not completely in accord with regard to Indonesian policy. Neither did the Japanese wish to place their considerable trade interests in Indonesia at risk. The British also felt that deep in their hearts, the Japanese saw the British as being clumsy in their handling of Indonesia, believing that they, as Asians, have a far better idea.[8]

As we can infer from this, the British realized they had limited influence over Japan and were seeking to influence its Indonesia policy through the United States. The best way to move Tokyo was through Washington. However, if the Japanese had noticed a discrepancy between the United States and United Kingdom, this approach would prove completely ineffective.

Moreover, as we shall see, the United States itself was about to try its hand at mediation. As if seeing through the gap between the United States and United Kingdom, Japan kept ignoring Britain's repeated requests, and knowing it could do nothing about this only increased British frustration.

The United States abandons Sukarno

In the following year, in early 1964, the administration of Lyndon B. Johnson, who had taken office following the assassination of President Kennedy, set out to mediate the Malaysian conflict. The move reflected the predicament in which the Johnson administration found itself. Why should America continue providing aid to Sukarno, who was bitterly opposed to the British, a staunch US ally? It had become difficult to push back the dissenters in Congress. But if the United States withdrew its aid, that would drive Indonesia toward the Chinese and Soviet camp. Furthermore, leaving the Malaysian conflict unchecked could get the United States directly involved through the invocation of the ANZUS Treaty.

To defuse the situation, Attorney General Robert F. Kennedy was appointed as special envoy in charge of mediation. Kennedy decided to seize the opportunity offered by Sukarno's visit to Japan in January 1964 and sought to persuade him in Tokyo. At the meeting, Sukarno said he would agree to a ceasefire if Malaysia also agreed, and having duly gained agreement from Malaysia, Kennedy set off to persuade the British.

Once back in Jakarta, however, Sukarno backtracked and began making statements urging the continuation of the confrontation with Malaysia, explaining that there would only be a change in tactics. When he returned to his country, Sukarno had been forced to heed the pressures placed on him by domestic groups such as the Communist Party of Indonesia, which were indignant about his acceptance of Kennedy's mediation.

Repeated consultations were held to hammer out the details of Kennedy's mediation plan, but talks broke down in the end over issues like the order in which the withdrawal of guerrillas and political consultations would take place. The United States hinted at reducing aid to put pressure on Sukarno, which only invited heightened objections. And in March, Sukarno, who had become increasingly frustrated by criticism within the United States, lashed out—pointedly, in English—in an excited outburst: "I have the following words for countries that offer aid with political strings attached: Go to hell with your aid!" This had sensational repercussions in the United States, where Congress and the public were outraged. The Johnson administration was left with no choice but to give up on a mediation effort that was going nowhere.

By this time, those who questioned the wisdom of past policy based on a conciliatory approach to Indonesia were gaining ground within the administration. According to their view, Sukarno's reasons for promoting confrontation with Malaysia were purely due to domestic political dynamics. If this was the case, negotiations were not going to stop him.

Meanwhile, Sukarno escalated his hard-line approach. In July 1964, large-scale riots between ethnic Malays and ethnic Chinese broke out in Singapore, which was now part of Malaysia, amid frictions with the federal government in Kuala Lumpur. Witnessing the confusion as it unfolded, Sukarno harbored the hope that Malaysia would quickly disintegrate if he kept up the heat. Sukarno stepped up military pressure on Malaysia by launching landing operations on the Malay Peninsula while vocally criticizing US policy on Asia and making the decision to recognize North Vietnam. For the first time, the Johnson administration could not help but feel a clear sense of discomfort toward Sukarno.

By the fall of 1964, the Johnson administration was preoccupied with its full-scale military intervention in Vietnam, which was now imminent. Due in part to these circumstances, America decided to give up on Sukarno's turnaround. Instead, the United States decided to pin its hopes regarding Indonesia on "post-Sukarno" developments and formulated a new policy that emphasized avoiding a collapse in its relationship with Indonesia during the interim. Meanwhile, full-scale US military intervention in Vietnam, which was a matter of great consequence for Asia, was about to produce a dynamic that would close the gap between the United States and United Kingdom. Around that time, America had abandoned the Ngo Dinh Diem government, which was subsequently overthrown in a coup d'état, leaving a hectic succession of administrations and frequent coup d'état attempts that further weakened the government. By early 1964, two-thirds of South Vietnam was under the control of the National Front for the Liberation of the South.

Concerned that submission to the Communists in South Vietnam would lead to similar developments in other parts of the third world, the Johnson administration prepared to send ground troops into Vietnam. However, faced with considerable objections to a full-scale military intervention both at home and abroad, it was becoming increasingly important for the administration to win the support of Britain—America's foremost ally.

Out of this situation emerged the dynamics of reciprocal support between the two countries, in which the British would support America in Vietnam while the Americans would support the British in the Malaysian conflict. In July, during Prime Minister Abdul Rahman's visit to America, Johnson declared US support for Malaysia and announced the start of military aid. The shift in the US approach was clear, and as a result, Japan's Indonesia policy of engaging Sukarno in step with the United States was shaken to its very foundations.

Amid these developments, Prime Minister Ikeda, who had led Japan's mediation efforts, stepped down following his crowning achievement of hosting the Tokyo Olympics in October 1964. Yet, even at his deathbed the following year, Ikeda continued to show a keen interest in Indonesia. He invited Indonesian Foreign Minister Subandrio to a meeting upon his visit to Japan to offer his advice, saying, "Sukarno may think the Communist Party is under control, but he will eventually be swept off his feet. You should tread carefully." And Subandrio, who was pushing for even closer ties with the Communist Party of Indonesia at the time, replied that he was "well aware."[9]

But the conditions that had been the prerequisites for Ikeda's mediation, such as Sukarno's pursuit of peace and the conciliatory stance of the United States, were disintegrating. Meanwhile, the Indonesian economy continued to deteriorate, due in part to the prolonged confrontation with Malaysia, and the Communists were rapidly expanding their influence.

Undertones of optimism were also being phased out of the Japanese Foreign Ministry's analysis of the situation. "Sukarno's political fortune is being sustained by addressing domestic needs that are better served by adopting a confrontational policy of creating external enemies to rally public support than by making a steady effort to build the economy," the ministry opined, offering little hope for a resolution of the Malaysian conflict in the immediate future. "Public discontent grows with no signs of abating, and Sukarno is facing the greatest difficulties the country has seen since it was founded."[10]

At the start of 1965, the Johnson administration would start bombing North Vietnam, while Sukarno would lead his country out of the United Nations and move rapidly closer to China by upholding the banner of the Beijing–Jakarta Axis. Under these circumstances, Japan was about to make its final effort at mediation. The initiative was led by Shojiro Kawashima, vice president of the LDP.

Final attempt at mediation—Shojiro Kawashima

The year was almost out the door when, on December 31, 1964, Sukarno suddenly announced that if Malaysia were to join the Security Council, Indonesia would leave the United Nations.

After attaining nationhood, Malaysia had joined the UN, and was scheduled to become a non-permanent member of the Security Council in January 1965. Sukarno, calling for the destruction of Malaysia, had refused to recognize the decision and was now saying his country would leave the UN. Withdrawal of a member was an unprecedented event in the history of the United Nations.

In Indonesia, the crises under the Sukarno regime were intensifying, as the decline in its economy gathered pace and as tensions mounted between the Communist Party, which was rapidly expanding its influence, and the army. And Sukarno's political style, in which he sought to withstand domestic tensions by creating an external crisis, had led to his ever-escalating hard-line stance against the outside world, exemplified by his threat of withdrawal from the UN.

Eisaku Sato, who had become prime minister following Ikeda's resignation, wrote that, in reaction to news of Indonesia's exit from the UN, he "felt somewhat agitated...then again, it did sound plausible."[11] Sukarno, who had earned the moniker "the roughneck of Asia," was now looked upon with detachment, even in Japan.

Sato thought of sending a special envoy to talk Sukarno out of leaving the UN, and the first name to come up was that of LDP vice president Shojiro Kawashima. At the time of the Tokyo Olympics, Indonesia had antagonized the International Olympic Committee on political grounds, and Kawashima, as the cabinet minister in charge, had handled the issue. He had befriended Sukarno during the incident and was counted among the Japanese politicians who were most closely connected to Sukarno at the time.

But persuading Sukarno to remain with the UN was inevitably linked to the Malaysian conflict, and would thus be equivalent to an attempt at mediation. As one of the few countries maintaining friendly terms with Indonesia, Japan was asked not only by the Johnson administration, but also by UN Secretary-General U Thant, to play its part in resolving the endless confusion of the Malaysian conflict.

However, considering that the Maphilindo plan and Robert F. Kennedy's efforts at mediation had both failed to bring about results, Japan would have to exercise caution. But an ideal opportunity for Japan to take the initiative presented itself on the diplomatic calendar: In April, a ceremony commemorating the tenth anniversary of the Bandung Conference was to be held in Indonesia.

Having Kawashima represent Japan at the ceremony would create a natural situation in which to seek contact with Sukarno. To be discussed was a proposal calling for the establishment of a mediation committee that would comprise four countries from Asia and Africa, which would be appointed by each Maphilindo country. The same plan had been discussed repeatedly during past attempts at mediation led by various countries. In essence, it hinged on whether Sukarno and Prime Minister Abdul Rahman of Malaysia would accept it.

Just before Kawashima left for Indonesia, Abdul Rahman changed his consistently passive stance and declared his willingness to accept the establishment of an Asian-African mediation committee. Behind Abdul Rahman's change of attitude lay the Second Asian-African Conference (the first being the Bandung Conference), which was to take place in Algiers, North Africa, in June.

Malaysia had expressed its wish to participate in this conference, but had met with stubborn opposition from Indonesia. In accepting mediation, Abdul Rahman's motive apparently lay in cultivating a favorable impression among the countries of Asia and Africa to facilitate Malaysian participation in the Algiers Conference. Whatever the reason, it was good news for Kawashima.

Once in Jakarta, Kawashima went in for a meeting with Sukarno. He persuaded Sukarno to meet with Abdul Rahman to discuss the establishment of the Asian-African mediation committee. He also pledged Japan's support for the Algiers Conference, on which Sukarno had focused much effort, and promised that he himself would attend as a delegate. On an economic note, Kawashima spoke of providing financial aid for building a thermal power plant.

The proposal clearly expressed Japan's resolve to continue supporting Indonesia even as the United States withdrew its support and the United Kingdom attempted to implement economic sanctions. It also closely reflected Japan's intentions of preventing Indonesia from becoming further radicalized and—as we will examine later—from gravitating toward China.

In response, Sukarno said he welcomed Japan's mediation with enthusiasm, stressing that he was ready to accept whatever solution was proposed. However, Kawashima could not deny that behind this positive attitude lay the same motive as Malaysia's: Appearing receptive to mediation in order to create a favorable impression ahead of the Algiers Conference. After leaving Indonesia, Kawashima visited Abdul Rahman and obtained his consent to a meeting with Sukarno in Tokyo.

Meanwhile, in Jakarta, Shizuo Saito, Japan's ambassador to Indonesia, met Sukarno to discuss the details of Kawashima's mediation plan and was confronted with an unexpected problem. According to official records, when Sukarno was informed about Abdul Rahman's willingness to meet him in Tokyo,

> [Sukarno] mentioned how Japanese magazines were publishing slanderous articles about his Japanese wife Dewi-san, and lashed out at the Japanese government for permitting magazines to insult a head of state. He apparently finds recent articles by Hirotatsu Fujiwara particularly offensive. Saito sought variously to appease him with words, but he [Sukarno] stubbornly insisted he would not go to Japan. Saito says he felt embarrassed that such a person could be a head of state.[12]

In November the year before, Dewi had attempted suicide during her stay in Japan, forcing Sukarno to send Foreign Minister Subandrio to persuade her to return to Indonesia, so there was certainly reason behind Sukarno's nervousness about her.

Saito promised to do everything he could to comply with Sukarno's wishes, which seemed to please the Indonesian leader. Saito, who had known Sukarno since World War II, said he had a premonition that "this time around, it might work out." In Tokyo, Chief Cabinet Secretary Tomisaburo Hashimoto gathered magazine reporters at Saito's request and asked them to exercise caution when writing about Dewi, since the situation was entering a delicate stage.

By the next morning, however, Sukarno's attitude had changed completely. Saito was asked to sit in on a cabinet meeting, where one of the ministers said: "While we may reinforce our policy toward Malaysia, easing it would be out of the question. This is the common will of the people." Sukarno then said: "Mr. Ambassador, as you have heard, this is the opinion of my key minister. Please accept it as Sukarno's response." He had effectively rejected Kawashima's mediation.

In spite of all this, Sukarno subsequently backtracked, saying he could meet Abdul Rahman in Tokyo depending on the date and format of the meeting. The Japanese government brought all pressure to bear,[13] which included sending a letter from Prime Minister Sato to Sukarno inviting him to Tokyo for a meeting with Abdul Rahman before the Algiers Conference in June. As noted above, Indonesia and Malaysia were engaged in a fierce tug-of-war over the Algiers Conference, each seeking to win the support of Asian and African countries. Irrespective of whether Malaysia would be allowed to participate, the relationship between the two countries was expected to deteriorate further once the conference was over, and that would make any summit meeting impossible. It was precisely for this reason that Japan asked Sukarno to meet Abdul Rahman before the Algiers Conference.

But June passed without Sukarno visiting Japan, and Kawashima's efforts ended in vain. Meanwhile, the Algiers Conference itself was postponed by a coup d'état that broke out in the host country Algeria and was eventually canceled.

So why did Sukarno behave in such a dubious manner at the time? Articles about Dewi may have played a part. But a more fundamental reason was that he had been standing at the final crossroads. He could choose to change his course slightly toward nation-building with economic support from free-world nations by accepting Japanese mediation and suspending the confrontation with Malaysia, or he could forge ahead down the radical path by stepping in line with the Communist Party of Indonesia and its backers in China.

The tug-of-war with China

In Indonesia, there had always been hostility toward its ethnic Chinese, who held the reins of the economy but were nevertheless viewed as being highly loyal to mainland China. And Indonesia's relationship with China was not exactly friendly, due to frequent frictions over issues involving its ethnic Chinese. However, as Sukarno sought to radicalize the struggle against colonialism by shifting the focus from the West Irian conflict to confrontation with Malaysia, China became one of only a handful of countries that consistently supported the Indonesian position.

For its part, China had antagonized India—the country with which it had once led Asia under the Five Principles of Peaceful Coexistence—through the Sino-Indian War, and by this time its disagreement with Soviet Russia had become public knowledge. China was criticizing the Soviet Union for being "revisionist," while emphasizing class struggle in its own diplomatic policy and thus facing international isolation, and Indonesia had become a dependable figure. In addition, the rapidly growing Communist Party of Indonesia had taken the Chinese side in the Sino-Soviet split, and China was encouraging the party to ally with Sukarno.

And so it was that Indonesia and China were brought together primarily by their radical political policies, in which ideology came foremost. China viewed the world in terms of a class struggle, while Sukarno saw it as a battle between the existing powers and emerging powers; as they upheld their campaign policies based on their respective world views, both China and Indonesia became isolated in the international community, emerging as perfect partners for each other. From late 1964 and into 1965, the leaders of these two countries began to pay frequent visits to each other, in what was to be called the Beijing–Jakarta Axis.

In April 1965, when Kawashima was making his attempts at mediation, the pressing issue for both China and Indonesia was the handling of the Algiers Conference, which was at that point two months away. Like Kawashima, Zhou Enlai and Foreign Minister Chen Yi traveled to Jakarta for the tenth anniversary of the Bandung Conference and stayed on after the ceremony to engage in repeated discussions with Sukarno and Subandrio, with the Communist Party of Indonesia acting as the go-between.

The upcoming Algiers Conference was of great significance to China. At this meeting, which was to be a gathering of Asian and African countries, China planned to strike out in explicit opposition to "American imperialism" and, furthermore, to seek permanent status for the conference, which would be organized around the idea of anti-imperialism and anti-colonialism. China would use this forum as a weapon to check the escalating US intervention in Vietnam. It would also give substance to the "intermediate zone" stressed by China as the focus of the international struggle, thus offering a counterweight to the Soviet Union, which acknowledged only the two major blocs of the United States and the Soviet Union. That would place China at an advantage in its ideological battle with the Soviet Union.

However, whether China would be able to accomplish its goals remained in the balance. At the time, non-aligned countries were involved in a fierce leadership battle. The movement was split between the "Conference of Non-Aligned Countries," a group led by India and Egypt that advocated a course of peaceful coexistence, and the "AA Conference" group led by China and Indonesia, which sought to control the Algiers Conference by advocating anti-imperialism, anti-colonialism, and anti-neocolonialism. While the AA Conference group sought to have its views on the border war between China and India, the Sino-Soviet dispute, and the Malaysian conflict reflected in the Algiers Conference, India was seeking to restrain the AA Conference group by inviting China's archrival, the Soviet Union, to Algiers for the conference.

For China to be able to seize control of the Algiers Conference by eliminating Soviet participation and achieve a breakthrough in its diplomacy, it was imperative that Indonesia—one of its few partners—should maintain a radical stance. But it was at this point that Kawashima began his mediation efforts. If Sukarno accepted his offer, China's diplomatic strategy would collapse. Newspapers affiliated with the Communist Party of Indonesia joined in a chorus of protests against Japanese involvement, publishing articles claiming that "the Indonesian people will not fall into the trap set by the monopolistic capitalists of Japan."

During a series of meetings with the Indonesian side, Zhou Enlai worked hard to convince Sukarno to postpone the settlement of the Malaysian conflict until June and pleaded with him to take the initiative in blocking Soviet participation in the Algiers Conference. Zhou explained to Sukarno that if he waited until the Algiers Conference, he would be able to seek a resolution to the conflict from a position of advantage backed by Asian and African countries.

When Sukarno replied that Indonesia's rapidly deteriorating socioeconomic situation would not allow him to wait until June, Zhou immediately offered to provide US$50 million in emergency aid and to deliver weapons equivalent to several military divisions as soon as possible. The idea was to use those weapons to form a "people's army of laborers and farmers" to address the issue of domestic security. And when Sukarno still withheld his response, Zhou told him China was not opposed to resolving the Malaysian issue and pressed further by saying he was "only suggesting a postponement" of any settlement until sometime in the fall of 1965, after the Algiers Conference.

In the end, Sukarno decided to go along with Zhou's proposal by postponing the resolution of the Malaysian confrontation and, as an obvious consequence, began to display a decidedly reluctant attitude toward Kawashima's mediation. Faced with this sudden change in Sukarno, Ambassador Saito said he "knew intuitively that a huge outside pressure had come down upon [Sukarno]."

"Phantom gift of the A-Bomb"

But by no means did Sukarno fully commit Indonesia's cause to China. Even as late as August, when Indonesia had moved closer to China, Sukarno told key cabinet members that Indonesia must strive to seek aid from all available channels to avoid being placed under the Chinese umbrella.

And yet, he ultimately set course in a direction that aligned the country with China. Furthermore, while Sukarno did receive consistent support from China as he became increasingly isolated in the international community, it cannot be denied that he had also become "fixated on the phantom gift of the atomic bomb from Communist China," according to Adam Malik, a politician who had been influential since Indonesia's independence and who served as vice president in the Suharto regime. In a speech made in July, Sukarno betrayed this fixation, saying, "God willing, Indonesia will shortly produce its own atomic bomb. It will not be used to invade other peoples or countries, but to guard our sovereignty against intervention from barbarians." A top officer in the army also stated publicly that Indonesia would conduct a nuclear test in the fall of the same year and that the Mentawai Islands, off the west coast of Sumatra in the Indian Ocean, had been selected as the test site.

The United States doubted it was possible for Indonesia to obtain nuclear weapons, but nonetheless began considering ways to minimize the political fallout if it should become a reality. Meanwhile, China, whose official stance was that it hoped to see many Asian and African countries obtain nuclear weapons, would have certainly considered using Sukarno's obsession to its advantage.

Even after this point, Kawashima continued to maintain his interest in mediation, but as Sato wrote in his diary, "only Mr. Kawashima seems enthusiastic." There was no longer any support in Japan for actively seeking involvement with Indonesia from a standpoint that was favorable to Sukarno.

"Sukarno has come under too much pressure in Indonesia to make his trip to Tokyo," an officer in the Indonesian army confided. Sukarno's political style was to maintain his leadership by deftly manipulating multiple elements—playing the Communists against the army at home while dealing with China, the Soviet Union, and the United States abroad. And as his juggling act neared its end, Sukarno was walking into a narrow alley that would limit his options. His day of reckoning—September 30, 1965—was fast approaching.

The extent to which the Japanese were aware that they were engaged in a tug-of-war against China over Sukarno's Indonesia is unclear. For instance, Japan's postwar relationship with China has frequently been explained as a process leading up to the resumption of diplomatic relations. On the other hand, there was certainly another angle, in which postwar Japan and China were the leading players, respectively, of the Eastern and Western blocs in Asia during the Cold War.

At the Bandung Conference, pro-Western countries such as Pakistan had invited Japan as the leading anti-Communist player in order to curb China's initiative. This clearly indicated that it was part of the reality created by the relative positions held by Japan and China in Asia, irrespective of any lack of self-awareness on the part of the Japanese. And as postwar Japan deepened its involvement in Asia by focusing on the economy, right in its path lay China, which was seeking to guide Asia down the alternative route of revolution.

While Indonesia was the anchor of maritime Asia, it was also a typical example of postwar nation-building in Asia; it was a region that had won its independence from colonial rule at the end of a bitter struggle that continued to pursue the path of creating a nation and its citizens out of a territory and its people with nothing in common except for their shared past under the rule of Dutch colonizers. In that sense, it was truly symbolic that Japan and China were engaged in a tug-of-war to draw Indonesia to its own side, seeking to influence its future.

The twilight of the British Empire

Around the time Japan and China were involved in their tug-of-war over Indonesia, the position of the United Kingdom, which had consistently taken a hard-line approach to Sukarno, was beginning to crumble. Despite British determination to protect it, Malaysia was on the brink of collapse.

At issue was the rivalry between the federal government under Prime Minister Abdul Rahman and the state government of Singapore led by Lee Kuan Yew, which had been incorporated into the federation. Singapore had developed as a free port, and the federal government did not appreciate its prominence in Malaysia. Discord between the two began with frictions over industrial and financial policies and eventually grew into a full-fledged political conflict.

At the root of the struggle was the fact that the federal government, led by ethnic Malays, saw Malaysia as a land belonging essentially to Malays and considered its ethnic Chinese and Indian citizens as mere immigrants who had arrived under British colonialism, whereas in Singapore—where most of the citizens were ethnic Chinese—Lee Kuan Yew championed equality for all ethnic groups. And while the federal government upheld the slogan "Malaysia for Malays" and aimed at improving the status of Malays who were at a disadvantage economically, Lee Kuan Yew began proposing "Malaysia for Malaysians" to encourage equal participation by all ethnic groups in federal politics. The disparity between the two views eventually became an issue that affected the very foundation of the multi-ethnic state of Malaysia.

In 1964, against the backdrop of this conflict, massive racial riots broke out repeatedly in Singapore. Abdul Rahman and Lee Kuan Yew met secretly and decided there was no other alternative than to separate Singapore from Malaysia to avoid the situation from becoming a catastrophe.

When the British caught wind of this move, however, they expressed strong opposition. For the British, the separation of Singapore was an unacceptable idea that would effectively acknowledge the failure of the Malaysia plan. Moreover, as this was happening, the United Kingdom was engaged in sporadic fighting against Indonesia to protect Malaysia. Yet Abdul Rahman and Lee Kuan Yew continued to meet secretly and made the decision to separate Singapore in August 1965, deceiving the British by giving them no prior notice. At this point, the Malaysia plan in its original sense had collapsed, necessitating a major shift in the United Kingdom's approach to Sukarno.

The United Kingdom was facing a financial crisis, and the cost of fighting the Malaysian conflict had become a heavy burden. As if aware of these difficulties, by 1965 Indonesia began to escalate its military pressure on Malaysia. The British expected Sukarno to pursue his policy of confrontation for several more years and had to concede that it was no longer possible to maintain British troops in Southeast Asia to counter this threat. A report compiled the previous year said that the United Kingdom must close its military bases in Singapore and Aden, Yemen, by 1970 in order to reduce its spending on national defense.

It was at this point that Singapore separated from Malaysia, and while the United Kingdom was disappointed, it also viewed this turn of events as an ideal opportunity for extricating itself from the muddled conflict with Indonesia. As the separation of Singapore would leave Malaysia in a vulnerable state, an early reconciliation with Indonesia was also necessary to prevent that country from stirring unrest in Malaysia and causing further fragmentation or collapse.

However, this shift in British policy was met with strong opposition from the United States, which had already launched its full-scale military intervention in Vietnam. There was concern that if the United Kingdom closed its base in Singapore and retreated from Southeast Asia while America remained preoccupied with Vietnam, it could give Indonesia and China an opportunity to spread their influence in the region under the banner of the Beijing–Jakarta Axis. Australia and New Zealand, which also favored a continued British presence, were similarly firm in their opposition.

Finding itself under such circumstances, the United Kingdom pinned its hopes on the Japanese initiative, which it had staunchly opposed until that point. Sometime around August 1965, the British proposed having Japan host a conference to discuss the future status of Malaysia and Singapore, to which Indonesia would also be invited. It would be a de facto peace conference for the Malaysian conflict.

This was a marked departure from the United Kingdom's past approach of avoiding Japanese intervention, and within the British government there was a mixture of expectation and concern about asking Japan to host such a conference. On the one hand, there was expectation that the Japanese, as they sought to play a leading role in resolving the conflict, would be delighted to gain the confidence of the British and would respond positively, thereby increasing the likelihood of the conference being realized.

On the other hand, there was concern that handing over leadership in Asia to Japan could consign the United Kingdom to a subservient role under Japan's regional leadership and that the British might no longer be able to exert any influence over Japan.

From what I was able to glean from unclassified documents, it is not possible to know just how much progress was actually made with respect to this plan. At any rate, in less than a month the September 30 Incident would take place, changing everything.

In retrospect, ever since the heyday of the British Empire, maritime Southeast Asia had in effect been "British seas" centered on Hong Kong and

Singapore. Today, even traces of such a past are difficult to find. We could say that one of the most dramatic changes that took place in this region in the postwar era was the exit of the British and their replacement with the re-entry of Japan.

Although the United Kingdom had continuously sought to avoid Japanese involvement in the Malaysian conflict, in the end it had no choice but to plan its retreat from that dispute, and from Southeast Asia itself, by entrusting Japan with leadership. This implies that the Malaysian conflict—which at times gave rise to intense rivalry between Japan and the United Kingdom, with the United States in between—was indeed a major turning point.

The United Kingdom sought to guide the situation to its advantage by endorsing Japan based on its prestige. But at the same time, it also feared that once it handed over the reins to Japan, it would never regain them. In their hesitation, the British had begun to envisage their exit from Asia as a quiet certainty.

At any rate, it is remarkable how maritime Southeast Asia in the early 1960s saw the interplay of various plans for regional realignment, including the Malaysia plan and the Maphilindo plan, while at the same time serving as a stage where outside forces—including the United States, China, Japan, and the United Kingdom—engaged in fierce rivalry. This reflected the fact that the region's post-colonial future had yet to be decided; the region was in the process of seeking an answer. And the turning point at which its unresolved outcome would be settled was the year of 1965.

Notes

1 "Secretary of state for air, Oct. 4, 1961," note, TNA, CAB 131/ 26, D(61) 66.
2 Masaya Ito, *Ikeda Hayato to sono jidai* [Hayato Ikeda and His Times] (Tokyo: Asahi Shimbun, 1985), 163–164.
3 Ibid., 168.
4 "Summary of the first meeting between Prime Minister Ikeda and President Sukarno (political issues)," September 27, 1963, Documents released by the Ministry of Foreign Affairs of Japan, Information Disclosure No. 2620.
5 *Yomiuri Shimbun*, September 27, 1963. "Second meeting between Prime Minister Ikeda and President Sukarno (political and economic issues)," September 28, 1963. Documents released by the Ministry of Foreign Affairs of Japan, Information Disclosure No. 2620.
6 "Regarding observations on the Japanese political situation," dispatch from Ambassador Furuuchi at the Japanese Embassy in Indonesia to the Minister of Foreign Affairs, March 26, 1963, Diplomatic Record of the Ministry of Foreign Affairs of Japan A'0209.
7 Diplomatic document of the British Foreign Office. Foreign Office (FO), Far Eastern Department, January 9, 1964, TNA, FO 371/ 176005 FJ 1022/ 3(B).
8 FO, Far Eastern Department, January 9, 1964, TNA, FO 371/ 176005 FJ 1022/ 3(B).
9 Mitsuo Taguchi, *Ajia wo kaeta kudeta: Indoneshia 9.30 jiken to nihon taishi* [The Coup d'etat That Transformed Asia: The 9.30 Incident in Indonesia and the Japanese Ambassador] (Tokyo: Jiji Tsushin-sha, 1984), 41–42.

10 "Current political and economic situation in Indonesia," Southeast Asia Division, August 1964, Diplomatic Record of the Ministry of Foreign Affairs of Japan A'4.1.0.5–4.
11 Eisaku Sato, *Sato Eisaku nikki* [Diaries of Eisaku Sato], vol. 2 (Tokyo: Asahi Shimbun, 1998), 218.
12 Indonesia Task Force, Diplomatic Record of the Ministry of Foreign Affairs of Japan A'0209.
13 "Djakarta to FO, May 15, 1965," Diplomatic document of the British Foreign Office, TNA FO 317/ 181500 IM1042/ 123.

4 The turning point of postwar Asia—1965

Figure 4.1 Indonesia's President Sukarno and Madame Dewi celebrating the completion of a hospital in Jakarta, December 10, 1965.

Source: © AP/AFLO.

The September 30 Incident—the mystery coup d'état

In March 1965, tensions gathering over Southeast Asia were about to reach a breaking point. In Vietnam, which continued to be a focal point not only for Southeast Asia but for postwar international politics, the US administration of President Johnson had finally decided to launch a major land offensive, and 180,000 soldiers were to be sent to Vietnam by the end of the year.

In Indonesia, which was the other focal point in the region, Sukarno had decided to consummate the Beijing–Jakarta Axis, and his "year of living dangerously" (as he had titled his National Day speech in the previous year) was headed for a climax.

In 1964, Indonesia was cut off from aid and trade by the escalating Malaysian conflict; the consumer price index had risen to 135 percent amid frenzied money printing and was set for a further surge in 1965. At the same time, military spending accounted for 50–70 percent of the national budget, leaving the economy in a critical condition. Throughout the country, the hair-trigger standoff between the Communist Party of Indonesia, which was relentlessly liberating land by force, and the army and Islamist groups that opposed the party was becoming more volatile.

In addition, the Communist Party was now demanding that a "Fifth Branch" militia be created by arming workers under its influence and that this body be allowed to intervene in military affairs through the establishment of a political committee within the national armed forces. For some time now, Zhou Enlai had been proclaiming the need for a "Fifth Branch," so it was not difficult to see the looming shadow of China behind the Communist Party of Indonesia. The precarious balance between the forces was giving way to a state of overwhelming tension.

Against this backdrop, Sukarno's collapse on August 5 immediately spawned rumors of a coup d'état. It was obvious that if anything happened to Sukarno, the delicate balance would snap, putting an end to the existing system. Meanwhile, it was also rumored that a cache of arms intended for the Communists was being secretly unloaded on the beaches of Java, Indonesia's main island. As the economy continued to unravel, tensions within Indonesia were approaching their limits.

By September, rumors of coup d'états and conspiracies led by right-wing and left-wing groups circulated through the streets of Jakarta every other day. While some claimed that Sukarno was dying from a chronic liver ailment, others said he had recovered completely. Toward the end of the month, rice—the dietary staple of Indonesians—temporarily disappeared from the shelves, provoking anxiety among citizens. "Something was about to happen. The streets of Jakarta were filled with a tense atmosphere that made it almost inevitable that something would happen."[1]

Finally, that moment came in the early hours of October 1. Jakarta was still enveloped in darkness when gunshots were heard in different parts of the city. As dawn broke, the citizens of Jakarta saw soldiers and tanks deployed at various locations. Something had obviously happened.

According to the radio broadcast, the "September 30 Movement" led by Lieutenant Colonel Untung bin Syamsuri, commander of the presidential guards, had set up a "Revolutionary Council," and troops under its command had attacked and abducted the top generals of the army, including Armed Forces Chief of Staff Abdul Haris Nasution and Army Chief of Staff Ahmad Yani. The kidnappings, which were explained as a move to preempt a coup d'état attempt by the generals against Sukarno, appeared to be an uprising in support of Sukarno.

However, the September 30 Movement was in control of the situation only for a day. Suharto, the commander of the Army Strategic Reserve Command (KOSTRAD), who had not been a target of the attack, launched a campaign to subdue the movement. Pushed back by soldiers commanded by Suharto, by the end of the day troops that sided with the movement were forced to withdraw to their stronghold at Halim Air Base outside Jakarta.

Meanwhile, following the initial report of the incident, Sukarno gathered further information and also moved to Halim Air Base. Top members of the Communist Party were there as well, which subsequently gave rise to suspicions regarding Sukarno's actions. The next day, the movement collapsed as the base was subdued; Communist leaders fled to the central regions of Java, and Sukarno moved to a presidential palace in the suburbs.

Sukarno subsequently returned to Jakarta, but consistently avoided criticizing the Communist Party of Indonesia, which was suspected of being the "mastermind" behind the September 30 Incident (so called due to the September 30 Movement that led the uprising, despite the fact that it occurred in the early hours of October 1), and tried to downplay the incident as "a ripple in the ocean of revolution." By doing so, Sukarno sought to maintain the balance of power that sustained his regime.

Soon the bodies of General Yani and the others, who had been murdered after being kidnapped, were discovered in an unused well. The process of recovering the bodies was televised nationwide, and the grand funeral that took place the next day was followed by an outpouring of public anger and sympathy for the dead generals. It was no longer possible to dismiss the incident as a mere "ripple." Meanwhile, Major General Suharto, who had played a key role in suppressing the insurgency, gained popularity by taking the lead in the funeral proceedings and calling for revenge against the perpetrators. He would eventually move to the center of the forces seeking to replace Sukarno.

The series of events that took place in the wake of the September 30 Incident not only led to a shift in power in Indonesia, but was to bring about a major turning point in postwar Asia.

Suharto's betrayal and unanswered questions

The case of the September 30 Incident is itself shrouded in mystery. As an uprising aimed at preventing a coup d'état that was itself suppressed, the incident is complicated enough in outline, while the circumstances that prevailed both inside and outside Indonesia and the interplay of various motives at the time have made it even more enigmatic.

As far as we know today, there is no evidence that a planned coup against Sukarno by the heads of the army ever existed. Nor is it possible to say that the Communist Party of Indonesia was behind the uprising. Since those who rose to action were leftist army officers under the influence of the Communist Party, the Communists had moved to take advantage of the uprising to deliver a blow to the army and gain the upper hand in the power balance.

How about President Sukarno? Like the Communist Party, he was probably aware that radical officers within the army were about to take some kind of action. Knowing this, he did not move to prevent it, calculating that he would be able to turn the situation to his advantage and maintain his hold on power by controlling both the army and the Communist Party. Yet, the abductions aside, the murder of the generals was a completely unexpected development for Sukarno, and the situation began to slip beyond his control.

While the ulterior motives of Sukarno and the Communist Party of Indonesia swirled about, the outcome of the situation was decided by the swift suppression of the uprising by Major General Suharto, which subsequently led to his rise to power and ascension to the presidency. In 1998, when the Suharto regime that had ruled for more than three decades collapsed in the wake of the Asian Financial Crisis, it was revealed that the September 30 Incident had played out against the hidden framework of a double coup d'état.

Suharto was able to launch a swift counterattack because he had escaped being attacked by the September 30 Movement, despite his position as a high-ranking member of the army. This was because he had been informed of the uprising beforehand by the movement and had given his tacit approval. Furthermore, by moving to wipe out the movement only after Commander Yani and the generals had been eliminated by troops under the movement, Suharto was able to declare his command over the army within a day of the incident.

Abdul Latief, who was a colonel at the time, was a leader of the movement who had informed Suharto of the planned uprising. Serving a life sentence since the September 30 Incident, Latief spoke out after the collapse of Suharto's regime. Latief said that Suharto

> probably gave his tacit approval to the plan because he had no hope of promotion as long as his superior, Commander Yani, and the other murdered generals remained. Mr. Suharto betrayed the national armed forces by failing to report to his superior officer, Commander Yani, and he betrayed us as well by suppressing us.[2]

There has been persistent speculation concerning the possible involvement of intelligence agencies of countries such as the United States and United Kingdom—which had found Sukarno difficult to deal with—or China, which had hoped the Communist Party of Indonesia would seize power. However, evidence to back up such claims has reportedly not been found.

Meanwhile, occasional testimony against the established theories, such as the aforementioned comment by Latief, has reinforced the sense of mystery that surrounds the September 30 Incident.

According to Fumihiko Kai, who was Japan's ambassador to Malaysia at the time of the uprising, Tunku Abdul Rahman, Prime Minister of Malaysia, confided the following information upon his visit to Japan in May 1965: In March of that year, a secret envoy from the Indonesian national armed forces had come to Abdul Rahman to inform him that they had a plan to eliminate Sukarno and the Communist Party soon and that the ongoing third-party mediation of the Malaysian conflict was doomed to fail because information was going straight to the Chinese side through Foreign Minister Subandrio, who was a China sympathizer. The envoy also instructed Malaysia to wait for the uprising by the Indonesian army.

Abdul Rahman asked Kai to relay this information directly to Prime Minister Sato, reminding him to keep the information from Shojiro Kawashima, who was close to Sukarno. Moreover, to indicate the authenticity of the information, Abdul Rahman had the content sent to Kai via an official dispatch from the Malaysian government. Kai, who went alone to the prime minister's residence to report to Sato, later stated, "Prime Minister Sato fixed his gaze on the copy of the official dispatch, and then gave a firm nod as if to say, 'I see. I understand.'"[3]

Shizuo Saito, who was ambassador to Indonesia during that same period, has said that he believes Kai's testimony to be founded on fact. Declassified diplomatic documents from countries belonging to the British Commonwealth confirm that Abdul Rahman also provided them with similar information. If Abdul Rahman's information was accurate, it would lend credibility to the claim made by the "September 30 Movement" that they sought to preempt a planned coup d'état by the army. Since these facts have come to light, Dewi has accused Sato of abandoning Sukarno to his fate despite having known of the incident in advance.

In a separate development, we now know from the memoirs of those who were involved that, prior to the September 30 Incident, the Indonesian army had developed a highly confidential channel with the Malaysian side behind Sukarno's back and had held repeated consultations to prevent an escalation in the military conflict. However, Abdul Rahman had apparently not been informed about this top-secret channel, and it is not clear whether it correlates to the aforementioned secret envoy sent by the national armed forces. In any event, this top-secret channel was to play a significant role in the process of ending the Malaysian conflict, which was led by the Indonesian army following the September 30 Incident.

"The greatest shock since Pearl Harbor"

Marshall Green, who was the US ambassador to Indonesia at the time of the incident, has said in retrospect that the September 30 Incident was the most shocking event in Asia since the attack on Pearl Harbor by the Japanese military.

It is certainly true that on the eve of the incident, Southeast Asia was about to be pressed in from the north and south by the Beijing–Jakarta Axis. The September 30 Incident turned the tables literally overnight. Where it had once been possible to envision a Communist takeover in the post-Sukarno era, the future of the "superpower of Southeast Asia" was now suddenly unpredictable.

The very fact that claims of clandestine American, British, and Chinese involvement in the September 30 Incident persist to this day indicates the magnitude of the incident's impact on the path taken by Asia in its aftermath. From the American and British perspective, things could not have turned out better; for the Chinese, on the other hand, it was an irrevocable blow.

Yet, however great the shock left by the incident, Sukarno remained alive and well. Now that the delicate balance between the Communist Party and the army had been broken, would Sukarno be able to maintain his grip on power in a country whose fate would have direct implications for Asian order, or would the army replace him? Following the incident, the United States, United Kingdom, China, and Japan became embroiled in an intense rivalry in what would effectively mark the final chapter in the competition over the outcome of decolonization.

One could argue that Japan had accomplished its "southward advance" by keeping Sukarno afloat. How did it respond to the outbreak of the September 30 Incident? Ambassador Saito in Jakarta initially expected considerable changes to come, but gradually leaned toward the view that Sukarno would bring the situation under control. Based on this assessment, the Japanese government sent a message to inquire after Sukarno about ten days after the incident. "I am very well, so please rest assured," Sukarno responded in Japanese. At this point, however, the only other countries that had sent messages welcoming his good health were Communist or pro-Communist countries such as China, the Soviet Union, North Vietnam, and North Korea.

The September 30 Incident diminished the influence of the Communist Party of Indonesia, thus tipping the balance of power firmly in favor of the army. Yet, having led the country for so long, Sukarno possessed superb political skills, and the diplomatic corps in Jakarta was divided in their opinion over the possible outcome of the developments.

The Japanese government was also divided in its reaction. On the one hand, it had sent a sympathetic message to Sukarno. But by mid-October—less than half a month since the incident—the Foreign Ministry in Tokyo had already begun considering the pros and cons of providing aid to the army. The key to the Indonesian situation, the ministry felt, was whether the army would be capable of taking on the role of government after securing law and order; this led them to conclude that "in the end, the army will have no choice but to seek foreign aid as a quick fix for the social unrest caused by concerns over the economy."

The ministry was clearly hoping that the military would seize power and was considering sending aid to support this scenario. During these discussions, it was also agreed that it would be difficult for Indonesia's military establishment to suddenly reverse the anti-US policy it had pursued under the Beijing–Jakarta Axis and seek aid from America. The United States, at any rate, lacked the capacity to respond, as it was engaged in a full-blown war in Vietnam, which consequently gave crucial importance to Japanese aid.

And even if Japan were to give the army support in the form of aid, it would at all costs have to avoid any appearance of intervention in Indonesia's internal affairs and uphold the principle of providing aid to a legitimate government. In addition, Japan was to avoid creating the impression it was biased toward the army by also informing the Sukarno side of its willingness to provide aid—though, as ministry officials concluded, "In view of his state of mind, it was unlikely that he would lend an ear to our recommendations."[4]

While this was all tentative, the speed with which Japan drew up its policy for supporting the army only days after the incident was evidence that the sense of discomfort toward Sukarno's radical policies had grown quite strong within the Japanese government, including the Foreign Ministry.

The expectations and reactions of each country

Sukarno continued to insist that while the September 30 Incident had been regretful, "incidents of this kind are bound to happen in a truly great revolution," and refused to criticize the Communist Party.[5] Over the years, the army had steadily gained power through rationalization and modernization, and Sukarno had long suspected it would one day seek his downfall. Sukarno's primary motive for encouraging the growth of the Communist Party lay in nurturing a countervailing force against the army. But now the Communist Party was on the brink of collapse—and the prospect of having to tackle the army singlehandedly was making Sukarno even more stubborn.

Japanese Ambassador Saito had hoped for a scenario in which Sukarno would oust the Communist Party and seek reconciliation with the army. Dewi also tried to persuade Sukarno to sever his ties with the Communist Party as quickly as possible to protect his status as the country's "founding father" and scrambled to set up an opportunity for a reconciliation with army leaders such as Suharto and Nasution, but Sukarno did not heed her advice.

Even then, Saito felt hesitant about abandoning Sukarno. Their friendship went back to 1942, when Saito was dispatched to Jakarta as a military government officer with the Java Expeditionary Force. It was there that he had first met Sukarno, the brilliant leader of Indonesia's independence movement. After being appointed ambassador, Saito gained an even stronger connection through Dewi and was even teased by other countries for possessing "a special entry pass to the presidential palace." However, it was precisely because of this close bond that Saito was at times criticized in Tokyo for being biased in favor of Sukarno when making decisions under the tenuous circumstances that followed the September 30 Incident.

When Saito returned to Japan in November, Prime Minister Sato gave the following instructions.

> From now on, I want you to be alert to any moves by the Soviet Union. If Communist China retreats and the Soviets make their advance, Indonesia could become the stage for Sino-Soviet rivalry, which would be a grave development...We must save Indonesia from its economic woes...When discussing aid, I want them to consider providing assurance that Japanese interests in their natural resources, such as oil and timber, will not be confiscated. And at this juncture it is also important to encourage them to support the private sector. In the past there was Kinoshita [Kinoshita Sansho Co., Ltd.], but it has since been absorbed by Mitsui [Mitsui & Co.], so please tell them to cooperate with Mitsui.

Sato went on to say, "I am dead set against Communism, so I want you to tell the Indonesian leaders that Sato is averse to Communism and the last thing he wants is the proliferation of Communism. You can mention me by name."[6] Sato's emphasis on eliminating Communist forces while securing and maintaining Japan's economic interests clearly indicated where Japanese priorities lay in the aftermath of the September 30 Incident.

Let us now turn to the reaction of the United States and United Kingdom. The crux of the American policy on Indonesia was above all to prevent it from becoming Communist. From this standpoint, it was a more than welcome development that the left-wing uprising had been crushed and the army had seized control in maintaining order. The question was whether the army could hold on to its advantage against an old hand like Sukarno.

Following the September 30 Incident, Sukarno had repeatedly implicated America in the affair. If the United States came out openly on the army's side, it would seem to substantiate Sukarno's claim that the incident had indeed been a US conspiracy, and could actually weaken the army's position. It was important not to appear as though the United States was meddling in Indonesia's internal power struggle, while at the same time letting key players in the army, such as Suharto, know that America was prepared to extend aid upon request.

Thus, while the United States hoped the army would seize power, offering its support would encourage the opposite outcome. Faced with this irreconcilable situation, the United States showed a keen interest in Japanese aid to Indonesia. The Americans expected Japan to respond positively if the army requested aid, noting how they "have a vital national interest in success of Army's campaign against PKI and in a stable and independent Indonesia." Nonetheless, an element of concern persisted: "Japan is still hypnotized by

Sukarno as the 'essential' man and they are being careful not to antagonize him."[7]

Nervous about the prospect of Japan siding with Sukarno, the United States began sending out feelers through various channels to determine the Japanese outlook while also seeking to communicate its own intentions. In addition to moves that were being made in Washington, Ambassador Reischauer met Ambassador Saito in Tokyo when the latter temporarily returned to Japan. The two agreed that Japan and the United States would maintain close contact on the Indonesian issue in order to stabilize the status quo—a situation that was more favorable to the free world countries than before the coup d'état. Saito pointed out that Japan should coordinate closely with America and other Western countries on providing aid to Indonesia. Reischauer replied that, since any overt move by the United States would have negative repercussions, Japan instead should lead other countries, including West Germany, the Netherlands, and Australia, as well as America.

Through these consultations, Japan and the United States gradually confirmed their shared understanding that they were not to extend any aid that would benefit the Sukarno side. However, while providing aid to Indonesia would be the most important means of bolstering the army, the question of which country should take the initiative emerged as a focal issue in handling the situation in Indonesia.

The United Kingdom had been carefully monitoring these developments from a different standpoint than that of Japan and the United States. The prime concern for the United Kingdom lay in extricating itself from the quagmire of the Malaysian conflict as quickly as possible; from this perspective, the developments that were unfolding in the aftermath of the September 30 Incident did not warrant optimism.

The British predicted that if Indonesia were to fall under the joint control of Sukarno and the army, it would definitely mean a continuation of the Malaysian conflict. On the other hand, if the army seized power, it could open the way to a resolution of the conflict. Conversely, however, it could also lead to an escalation in the confrontation with Malaysia as a means of uniting the country under the army. The latter scenario would force the United Kingdom to launch a full-scale military campaign in Malaysia, which would truly be a nightmare.

The United States, prioritizing countering Communism, pinned its hopes on the army, while the United Kingdom sought an earliest possible resolution of the Malaysian conflict. The difference in their positions introduced a subtle tension to the bilateral relationship. The Americans suspected that the British, in seeking an early resolution to the Malaysian conflict, might take advantage of the confusion to launch a military attack against Indonesia. The United States could not tolerate any attack that might undermine the Indonesian army's sweep operations against the Communists from behind. After several consultations, the United States and United Kingdom agreed to place top priority on destroying the Communist Party of Indonesia and to secretly assure the Indonesian army that the British Commonwealth forces would not attack Indonesia while the army was dealing with the Communists.

At the same time, the United Kingdom strongly insisted that aid to the Indonesian army should be linked to the discontinuation of its confrontation with Malaysia. In other words, an end to the Malaysian conflict was to be the precondition to any aid. From the British point of view, however, America and Japan were primarily interested in defeating Communism in Indonesia and did not seem too keen on resolving the Malaysian conflict. For the United Kingdom, it was imperative that other countries—and especially America—endorse its policy of making aid dependent on an end to Indonesia's confrontational policy against Malaysia. The British felt that there was a need to coordinate the policy on Indonesia among the four affiliated countries—the United Kingdom, United States, Australia, and New Zealand—and sought to move them toward that goal.

Mass murder and the collapse of the Communist Party

Having suppressed the September 30 Incident, Suharto launched a national campaign to weed out the Communist Party. In the rural areas, longstanding hostilities were about to explode between the communists, who were forcibly liberating land, and the landowners and Islamist organizations protesting these actions. With arms supplied by the army, attacks against individuals connected to the Communist Party turned into a massive wave of killings that engulfed the nation. The Communist leaders had pinned their hopes on a political settlement initiated by Sukarno and did not put up much of an organized resistance. Thus unhindered, the campaign claimed as many as 600,000 lives—even by estimates provided by the army in later years, making it, according to a CIA report, "one of the worst mass murders of the twentieth century."

The Foreign Ministry in Tokyo also received graphic accounts describing how the anti-Communist side was coming down on the Communist Party forces. In Bali, for example, they were

> surrounding and attacking them, starting with army gunfire, followed by the masses setting fire and killing, leaving the village mostly destroyed with seven thousand dead or injured…Arson and murder took place or are taking place throughout the island, bringing the number of dead or injured to 15,000 on the island alone.

Since it was believed that the Communist Party of Indonesia was backed by China—or that its supporters included many ethnic Chinese—the Chinese Embassy was burnt to the ground, and the ethnic Chinese population in Indonesia was also targeted for attack. And while the Chinese government repeatedly protested through diplomatic channels and through Radio

Beijing, this only aroused further resentment that led to an escalation in violence against the ethnic Chinese.

Yet the mass murders that went on for about half a year received little international attention at the time, and no country other than China offered much of a response. Parties from various countries who were involved at the time have cited reasons such as a lack of direct confirmation of the events. But as US Ambassador Green eventually revealed, calling for a halt in the fighting amidst the intense power struggle between the army and the Sukarno-affiliated Communist Party side was likely to only benefit the latter. And even if it were possible to determine the actual extent of the mass murders, as long as they ensured the destruction of the Communist Party that had guided the leftward shift in Indonesia, they were perhaps considered a tragedy that could be tolerated by governments, including those of Japan and the United States.

As the country's "founding father," Sukarno repeatedly ordered the army to stop the mass murders, but to no avail; the killings continued. Sukarno had spent his entire life seeking to unite the peoples and lands of Indonesia, which shared nothing but their past under the rule of Dutch colonialists, to create one nation and one people. He had staked everything on achieving independence and creating an integrated Indonesia, yet all he could do now was to sit and watch as it unraveled before his eyes.

With the collapse of the Communist Party, the political balance that had sustained Sukarno's immense authority and credibility fell apart, and the army would no longer listen to him. When Sukarno repeated his call for continuing the confrontation with Malaysia and consummating the Indonesian revolution, it no longer roused the people into a nationalist fervor. The Sukarno magic that had captivated his people was now gone.

And so, by the end of 1965, the army was mostly done routing the Communist Party throughout the country and had seized control of national order. Hamengkubuwono, the Sultan of Yogyakarta, who enjoyed great prestige among the Indonesian people, and the nation's technocrats were flocking to the side of the army and were beginning to draw up a concrete political vision. It was becoming clear that the forces aligned with the army were venturing beyond merely criticizing Sukarno and were now seeking to replace him. The situation seemed to be gradually moving in favor of the plan that was being considered by Japan and the United States—that is, providing emergency aid to bolster the army in its quest for power.

Support for the military takes shape

Throughout this period, a plan for sending aid to Indonesia was taking shape within the Japanese government so that immediate action could be taken once the right moment arrived. In early November, Japan formulated an extensive plan based on its support for the army's rise to power that went beyond bilateral relations and envisioned the development of a broad framework for providing aid to Indonesia with the participation of the countries concerned.

Here, the idea was that supporting the army's ascent to power would provide Japan with the advantage of securing its economic interests and, proceeding from there, solidifying its base for the future expansion of the economic relationship between the two countries. Furthermore,

> in view of the special nature of the situation in which major free-world countries lack conducive diplomatic relations with Indonesia, it is only natural for Japan to take the initiative, and is expected to be well received by Western countries as well as Indonesia.[8]

More specifically, Japan would pay due consideration to the radical nationalism and anti-colonial sentiment that existed in Indonesia and seek to avoid creating an impression that the country was being placed under international management by keeping the World Bank and the IMF out of the aid framework, "avoiding the image of multilateral aid as much as possible and making it appear as if we were responding to a self-initiated approach from Indonesia." Moreover, the principal countries extending aid would initially comprise Japan and other countries whose political relationships with Indonesia were not under strain, such as West Germany and France, while securing US support at the same time. Meanwhile, the Indonesian army would be asked to set up a "brain trust" to formulate a plan for economic reconstruction.

At this point, an important issue presented itself—the timing of extending aid. From the Japanese standpoint,

> whether the ongoing campaign to eliminate the Communist Party from Indonesia ends in success or failure will not only have grave consequences for the future of Indonesia, but is also a vital issue that could mark the turning point of whether Communism will expand throughout the Southeast Asian region or not. Seizing the moment to extend this emergency aid would be an effective move against the spread of Communism in Southeast Asia.[9]

Thus, Japan stressed the international significance and importance of its aid. However, Japan had been informed by none other than the Indonesian army leadership itself of their concern that Japanese aid would be snatched up by the Sukarno side.

In the end, Japan concluded that in deciding when to offer its aid, it was essential to seize the moment when the army had established control over the central government, asserting, "There is no other indicator to determine such a moment than when Deputy Prime Minister Subandrio is purged."[10] Around this time, the Japanese government had also received a request for aid from the Sukarno side, but it decided not to comply. Even Saito in

Jakarta was beginning to give up on Sukarno, who continued to reject reconciliation with the army. By now, it was evident that the Japanese government had adopted a stance of distancing itself from Sukarno.

The standoff between Sukarno and the army continued, and by the end of 1965 the economy was in dire straits as Indonesia ran out of foreign currency. This was accompanied by a dramatic increase in unpaid debts from Indonesia's trade with Japan. Finally, in late December, remittances from Bank Negara Indonesia ceased, triggering a suspension of Japan's export insurance for Indonesia, as it became impossible to collect export payments.

These events brought trade between Japan and Indonesia to a virtual standstill. Emphasizing the importance of Japan's relationship with Indonesia, the Foreign Ministry had argued against taking such a drastic step as suspending export insurance, but was overridden by the Ministry of Finance and the Ministry of International Trade and Industry, which insisted on applying the proper rules.

While Japan was the first country to adopt the tough measure of suspending trade insurance, Indonesia was similarly indebted to Western countries, the Soviet Union, and Eastern European countries; unless fundamental steps such as a moratorium on debt repayment were taken, sooner or later its foreign trade would dry up and its economy could crash. Due to this unexpected development, aid to Indonesia quickly became a pressing issue. Japan had counted on the purge of Subandrio, the top-ranking leftist in the government, but even before that scenario came to pass, the economic situation had deteriorated to a point that could no longer be ignored.

Japan dispatched a senior foreign ministry official to grasp the actual condition of the Indonesian economy, but even Bank Indonesia, the country's central bank, was in a state of confusion as it sought to accurately calculate the amount of foreign debt. The inspector's report stated that, while "the country's economy has deteriorated beyond the point where recovery is possible through normal means and requires a fundamental solution," the economic policy division of the Indonesian government was "taking things one day at a time as everyone awaits a 'political' solution…Under these circumstances it would be difficult to expect them to formulate a plan for new loans."

To resume trade with Indonesia, it was necessary to provide fresh loans, and obtaining approval from the Ministry of Finance and others within Japan required the Indonesian side to present a convincing plan for economic reconstruction. However, there was no hope for any well-thought-out economic reconstruction plan to be produced under the current political situation in Indonesia, where the bureaucracy could do nothing but await the outcome of the power struggle between Sukarno and the army.

Moreover, the Indonesian army had reiterated its position of not wanting Japanese aid while the power struggle with Sukarno continued. Meanwhile, Japanese industries that were largely dependent on trade with Indonesia, such as the import-export and textiles businesses, were calling for a resumption of trade.

America was alert to the possibility that the Japanese government might be pressured into extending aid to Indonesia by its domestic industries, even at the expense of defying the army's wishes. In fact, discussions were already taking place within the Japanese government for an aid policy that would allow for the resumption of trade with Indonesia, with a primary focus on rescuing Japanese industries. It appeared that Japan–US cooperation over Indonesia might break down.

Just then, the political situation in Indonesia took a major turn—in the opposite direction than the one expected by Japan and the United States. On February 21, Sukarno dismissed Nasution, a core member of the army, from his post as minister of defense and security. Sukarno had opted for a path of all-out confrontation with the army in what the Foreign Ministry of Japan called a "desperate counterattack."

However, Sukarno's decision was met by strong protest within Indonesia. Demonstrators surrounding the presidential palace grew in force with the backing of the army, and the target of their resentment began to shift away from Subandrio toward Sukarno. The city of Jakarta was enveloped in a sense of turbulence, and on March 11, while Sukarno was holding a cabinet meeting at the presidential palace, word came that the place was being surrounded by unidentified troops. This was followed by a report that their aim was to arrest Subandrio. Hearing this, Sukarno and several leftist ministers, including Subandrio, escaped by helicopter to Bogor Palace.

As if in pursuit, Suharto dispatched three of his trusted generals to Bogor, and they pressed Sukarno to dissolve the Communist Party, reshuffle the cabinet, and lower the price of commodities. Next, they demanded the handover of presidential authority to Suharto while guaranteeing Sukarno's personal safety. Sukarno resisted, but by evening he was forced to sign a presidential order—subsequently referred to as the "March 11 Executive Order"—that gave in to these demands. It was, in effect, a bloodless coup d'état by the army.

Suharto lost no time; the next day he outlawed the Communist Party and arrested fifteen leftist cabinet members, including Subandrio, while setting up a cabinet that reflected his policies. Sukarno protested that he had not delegated such extensive powers, but it was a futile effort.

The Japanese government had strongly hoped for a military takeover and openly welcomed Sukarno's decline when presented with this sequence of developments, noting that

> Sukarno's political strategy was to undermine the need for addressing economic woes with the rallying call of 'accomplishing the Indonesian revolution come hell or high water,' but it was all bark and no bite, as symbolized by monuments and impractically grandiose buildings; it has fallen out of favor with the masses and is becoming a thing of the past.[11]

Once it attained power, the Indonesian army promptly requested that Japan send emergency aid. In response, the Japanese government decided to send rice and clothing as the first shipment of emergency aid. To ensure that the military's rise to power was welcomed by the general public in Indonesia, it was important to create improvements that were visible to citizens; rice and clothing were expected to have an immediate impact.

Yet, having only just seized power, receiving highly publicized aid from Japan could still invite criticism against the army from leftist quarters. Upon consultation, it was decided that this would take the form of a grant aid through the Japanese Red Cross for damages incurred by large-scale flooding in central Java.

Japan's decision to send emergency aid opened the way for the United States and other countries to begin offering emergency assistance. And as aid from various countries began to arrive, a new, military-led Indonesian government was formed after eliminating the leftist factions, proclaiming the reconstruction of the domestic economy as its top priority.

But the Indonesian economy was on the brink of collapse, and reconstruction was hampered by the unavoidable issue of creating a framework to deal with the country's massive debt owed not only to Japan and Western nations, but also to a broader array of countries, including the Soviet Union and Eastern European countries with which Indonesia had been forging closer ties under the Sukarno regime. This marked the beginning of a new round of political bargaining, in which the interests and motives of various countries intertwined as they sought to establish an advantageous relationship with post-Sukarno Indonesia.

The United Kingdom and its final quest

As we have seen, Japan and the United States were hoping that power would fall into the hands of the Indonesian military, and Japan had been carefully watching for an opportune moment to begin providing aid to support this scenario. But the Indonesia policy adopted by Japan and the United States was causing growing concern in the United Kingdom. Placing top priority on resolving the Malaysian conflict, the British advocated linking Indonesian aid to the resolution of the Malaysian conflict and sought to win support for this policy from America, Australia, and New Zealand by inviting these three countries to a meeting in November, about two months after the September 30 Incident.

America suggested adding Japan—which it believed should play a central role in supporting Indonesia—to the meeting, but was met by strong objections from the United Kingdom. In the view of the British Foreign Office, the purpose of the meeting was to gather the United Kingdom, the United States, Australia, and New Zealand to formulate a policy that would benefit these four countries; there was no need even to inform Japan of the existence of such a meeting. The British aim was to hold prior consultations on basic policy with its closest English-speaking allies to secure its advantage in subsequent developments; within such a scheme, Japan was no more than an outsider.

In the end, America did not insist on inviting Japan. The United States was most concerned about keeping knowledge of the meeting itself a top secret. This was a gathering of English-speaking countries such as the United States and United Kingdom—in all appearances a "white man's club"—that was meeting to discuss how they should handle Indonesia; if it should become known to the Indonesians, it was certain to ignite their acute sense of nationalism. America had decided that Japanese participation would pose too great a risk to maintaining secrecy.

During the secret four-nation talks that took place in London in early December, the British argued that the United Kingdom and United States should contact the Indonesian military leadership to ascertain their true intentions regarding the Malaysian conflict. If they were seeking to escalate the conflict, the British response would be to apply military pressure to put an end to the confrontation policy. The United Kingdom needed to extricate itself from the quagmire of this conflict as quickly as possible, even if it meant considering a hard-line military option.

The other three countries were reluctant, however. The majority opinion was that it would be unwise for the United States and United Kingdom to seek contact with the Indonesian military while the power struggle with Sukarno continued; they should wait until the right moment presented itself. Faced with this response, the British began to suspect that perhaps America and Australia felt it was more convenient for their interests to have the Malaysian conflict continue.

It was around this time that the United Kingdom, under financial stress, had accelerated the pace of planning for a withdrawal from its base in Singapore. However, America, which was fighting the war in Vietnam, and Australia, which had also sent troops to Vietnam, opposed the planned withdrawal. They were deeply concerned about the disappearance of British military presence from Southeast Asia at a time when they were still engaged in war. Britain suspected the United States and Australia of thinking it would be to their benefit to have the Malaysian conflict continue as a low-level military conflict in order to retain the British forces in Singapore.

Unable to achieve its desired goal, the United Kingdom understood that the end of the Malaysian conflict was, as British diplomatic documents put it, "an insignificant and secondary issue" to the United States. This was also evident in the fact that the United States—placing greater weight on countering Communism—had begun to turn its attention from aligning itself with the United Kingdom to seeking cooperation with Japan and West Germany as countries capable of providing aid to Indonesia.

To secure its national interests, the British sought to manage the region among "family members"—the United States, Australia, and New Zealand. But the strategy was being eroded from its very foundations due to the United Kingdom's own decline, as symbolized by its planned withdrawal from Singapore that led to a weakening of the British position. Six years later, in 1971, the United Kingdom dissolved the British Far East Command in Singapore, which had been its longstanding base in Asia.

Contrary to British fears, once the Indonesian military had seized power through the March 11 Executive Order, the Malaysian conflict began to move toward a rapid resolution. With the backing of the Indonesian military, which had maintained contact with the Malaysian side from before the September 30 Incident, repeated consultations were held between Adam Malik, Indonesia's newly appointed foreign minister, and the Malaysian side. This enraged Sukarno, who wanted to continue the confrontation with Malaysia, but assured by the support of Suharto and the army leadership, Malik pressed on to normalize diplomatic relations. In August 1966, a formal peace treaty was signed, ending the Malaysian conflict. Subsequently, Indonesia and Malaysia went on to sign a Security Arrangement in the Border Regions in March 1967 and a Basic Agreement on Trade and Economic Relations in May of the same year, thus gradually normalizing their relationship.

And in August 1967, ASEAN was established. The formation of this new regional organization would not have been possible without the decline of Sukarno in Indonesia and the reconciliation with Malaysia that followed. Sukarno, the nationalist who gave his life to the "consummation of independence," and the United Kingdom, the colonial master that had become his target, were both gone from the seas of Southeast Asia, across which the winds of a new era stirred.

"A superb opportunity for encouraging steady development"

Although the political aspect of the turmoil in Indonesia that followed the September 30 Incident was resolved by the army's rise to power, the economic situation continued to deteriorate. Since money had been printed freely without the supply of actual goods under the Sukarno regime, by 1965 the country was in the grips of escalating inflation that caused a fivefold increase in general prices from the previous year, while the price of rice had surged ninefold. In 1965, foreign debt amounted to as much as US\$2.35 billion, but since only a small part of those funds had been spent on boosting production, which remained below 20 percent of capacity in early 1966. The economic crisis was not a transient phenomenon, but a structural condition that had accumulated under the Sukarno regime.

Sukarno was a politician who lived only for the dream of revolution. Unfortunately, as in the aftermath of a grand banquet, the dream faded away, only to leave behind a huge debt and an economic crisis. How could this negative legacy be resolved so as to place the Indonesian economy on a path to recovery? Reflecting Sukarno's neutralist policy, a significant portion of the debt was owed to the Soviet Union and Eastern European countries, as well as to Western countries; this necessitated an extensive international framework for seeking a solution.

Here, the issue focused on whether debtor nations were to separately engage in bilateral negotiations with Indonesia to provide aid that included debt consolidation, or whether they should all participate in a scheme based on a multinational consortium. Japan would aggressively push for the formation of a consortium in which countries moved in step, and it had clear reasons for doing so.

Japan's trade with Indonesia had been suspended by Indonesia's delayed debt payments and the suspension of trade insurance. One effective means of breaking through the situation and resuming trade was to allow the refinancing of Indonesian debt and the deferral of its payments.

However, to refinance loans extended by the Export-Import Bank of Japan—which accounted for most of Japan's loans to Indonesia—the Export-Import Bank of Japan Act stipulated that other major creditor nations must adopt similar measures as a precondition. Thus, in order to resume full-scale trade with Indonesia, Japan was under pressure to begin consultations with other creditor nations as soon as possible.

But countries approached by Japan about holding talks on Indonesian debt were not necessarily receptive to the idea. The Dutch did not want to jeopardize their relationship with Indonesia, which had begun to show signs of improvement, by joining an international effort, while West Germany felt quite capable of handling the issue through a bilateral effort because it was not bound by any rules like those of the Export-Import Bank of Japan Act.

Furthermore, Japan was pressing Indonesia to prioritize repayment of the short-term loans that accounted for much of Japanese debt; this was met with strong objection from Western countries whose loans were mostly mid- to long-term. From the beginning, consultations among creditor nations were showing signs of becoming a forum where each country sought to outmaneuver the others to gain a practical advantage. Were negotiations to be conducted bilaterally, or through the consortium scheme? Political bargaining between countries over the framework for providing economic aid to Indonesia seemed to drag on with no signs of reaching a consensus.

Among these countries, America had consistently taken the position that full-scale support for Indonesia would only function effectively under a multinational framework. Bilateral aid was often motivated by the respective interests of each country, and the United States felt it would hamper the fundamental reconstruction of the Indonesian economy, which would involve scaling down and raising the efficiency of a government structure that had become bloated under the Sukarno regime.

Yet the United States did not take the initiative on this issue and, instead, urged Japan to convene a meeting of creditor nations based on the consortium scheme. Sukarno was clearly anti-US and, though he had lost his grip on power, still held the position of president. Meanwhile, some measure of uncertainty remained with respect to the army's attitude toward America. For these reasons, the United States believed it was still risky to openly take the lead.

In Europe, the British encouraged the Germans to take the initiative on the issue, but failed to obtain a positive response. Under these circumstances, Japan resolved to host a meeting between Indonesia and its creditor nations in Tokyo. If realized, this would mark the first major international conference convened on Japan's initiative since the end of the World War II. However, the intentions of some countries in Western Europe remained unclear, and there were visible signs of anxiety within the Japanese government concerning the realistic prospects of such a conference taking place at Japan's initiative. Seeing this, the United States not only endorsed Japan's efforts to organize the meeting, but clearly expressed its intention to offer indirect support.

Deterred by their respective interests, Western European countries approached by Japan were reluctant at first, but gradually began to take a positive attitude toward the idea of holding a meeting of creditors. They had undeniably been influenced by the United States, which was encouraging each country to participate. By May 1966, West Germany and the Netherlands had followed the US lead and declared their support for resolving the issue through a meeting of creditors. Meanwhile, there was growing consensus on leaving the Soviet Union and the Eastern European countries out of the conference.

At the Foreign Ministry in Japan, work had begun on formulating a concrete policy for the conference of creditors. Here, we can see a sense of elation among the Japanese; military conflicts in Southeast Asia were viewed as being ultimately rooted in the slow pace of economic development and mutual mistrust. "Apart from reparations and related payments," ministry officials reported,

> no significant effort has been made to provide financial support for the Southeast Asian nations, and as the end of reparations and related payments approaches in many of these countries, there are great expectations of economic cooperation from our country as the only advanced nation in Asia.

They went on to note, "Recent international developments have shown that politics of the kind that ignores domestic development are receding among less developed countries, which presents us with a superb opportunity for encouraging these countries toward steady development."[12]

Here, we see no vestiges of the Japan that had once stood transfixed in bewilderment amidst the rush of Asian nationalism at the Bandung Conference. Secure in its robust economic growth, Japan did not hesitate to define itself as the "only advanced nation in Asia." Such confidence was inextricably linked to the view that the political emphasis was about shift to domestic development, opening the way for Japan to engage.

Asia's aspiration for "independence" had found an outlet at Bandung in the past, but its unifying force was lost with the decline of colonialism, while the "founding fathers"—epitomized by Sukarno—who had sought above all else to consummate the drive for independence were now making an exit all over Asia.

While seeking to expand its economic horizons, Japan also recognized economic development as the key to Asian stability, and the situation seemed to present a fine opportunity for spreading the wave of economic development throughout Asia. Japan's overflowing sense of confidence and elation was perhaps a reflection of its subconscious awareness that, as Asia was approaching a major turning point in its history "from decolonization to development," Japan had its finger on the very pulse of this great movement.

Here again, Indonesia was seen as the crucial link.

> For various reasons, our relationship with Indonesia is vastly closer than our relationship with Vietnam, which is another focus of attention in Southeast Asia. While allowing for some exaggeration, we could say that just as the United States is committed to Vietnam, we are committed to Indonesia, and therein lies the significance.[13]

In retrospect, the ministry noted that even when Sukarno began to gravitate toward Beijing and Japan feared it could no longer keep up with Indonesia, Japan had taken a long-term perspective and patiently and steadfastly continued its efforts to maintain Indonesia's ties with free-world nations, and such efforts were now being rewarded. Communist China had made spectacular inroads through its continuous penetration campaign, but following the sudden collapse of its foothold in Indonesia, Japan's presence in the country became hugely significant, placing it in the international spotlight. "It is not too much to say that the time has come for us to ensure our influence in the country and to offer our considerable contribution to ensuring stability throughout Southeast Asia."[14]

Yet Japan was also aware of the limits of its influence. "It goes without saying that we alone cannot support Indonesia. We need the cooperation of America and the other free world countries, and should therefore take the initiative to develop such a cooperative framework."[15] This cooperative framework was to take shape with the meeting of Indonesia's creditor nations, which represented an opportunity to draw the Western countries into supporting Indonesia.

The advent of the "era of development"

In September 1966, the meeting of Indonesia's creditor nations opened in Tokyo. The eleven participating countries included Japan, the United States, the United Kingdom, France, West Germany, Italy, the Netherlands, and Australia. At the meeting, Japan suggested starting with the rescheduling of payments for short-term debt that were due within a short period, setting aside the framework for long-term loan repayment that was expected to take some time to hammer out, and emphasized the need for fresh loans. In contrast, Western European countries advocated forming a concrete method of debt repayment before discussing new loans. While Japan sought to revitalize its economic relationship with Indonesia through new loans, the Western European countries were eager to settle the debts that had accumulated over the Sukarno years; this difference in their motives was apparent from the onset.

The meeting ran into difficulties, in part because the economic plan presented by the Indonesian government—which was to be the receiving end of new loans advocated by Japan—proved unconvincing. A basic agreement was nevertheless reached, approving a temporary waiver on payments for short-term loans that were due by the end of 1967. The remaining issues were to be discussed in Paris in December. It was not until 1970 that a final agreement was reached on the repayment method for debt acquired before the establishment of the Suharto regime.

We could say that the significance of the meeting of Indonesia's creditor nations actually lay in its political achievement. Upon its closing, a joint communiqué was released, in which the participating countries recognized the urgent need to alleviate Indonesia's massive debt burden and declared their confidence in "the Indonesian economy's capacity for recovery, the Indonesian government's resolve to implement its economic reconstruction plan, and the outlook for a rapid expansion in normal trade based on cash settlement."[16]

While the Vietnam War commanded the world's attention, in the other focal point of Indonesia, the anchor of maritime Asia, the Western countries had reaffirmed the significance of the establishment of a new military-led government that had parted ways with China and the Communist camp and had declared their political intention of providing as much support as possible in order to prevent a reversal of the situation and ensure stability.

A framework for providing aid to Indonesia was formed by the Western countries at this creditors' meeting, and it was to develop into an international mechanism for sustaining Indonesian development, which was about to be launched on a major scale under the Suharto regime.

Indonesia was a typical example where the new political trend of emphasizing a "system of development" manifested itself, where priority was placed on the pursuit of development over the consummation of independence. This trend spread among Southeast Asian countries starting in the latter half of the 1960s; the introduction of both foreign aid and private capital were essential to constructing and promoting such a system.

The framework created by the meeting of Indonesia's creditors provided a multilateral system of support that served as a "vessel" for promoting the developmental system built under the Suharto government. Much of what filled that vessel was to come from advances made by Japanese companies and aid extended by the Japanese government.

As Japan gradually eased its rules on direct foreign investment, Japanese companies launched their full-scale advance overseas, and by the first half of the 1970s, the amount of Japanese investment in Southeast Asia had shown an explosive ninefold increase compared to the latter half of the 1960s. Meanwhile, extension of foreign aid by the Japanese government also grew dramatically after 1965, and the lion's share of this aid went to Asian countries. Among them, Indonesia was the top beneficiary, receiving a cumulative total of US$18.223 billion by 2001—far outpacing China, which came in second with US$15.934 billion, and the Philippines, which received US$9.442 billion.

Seen from the Indonesian side, nearly half of all official development aid it received came from Japan alone, accounting for a considerable portion of its development budget. In that sense, it would not be an exaggeration to say that any "development" that was undertaken under the Suharto regime would not have been possible without aid from Japan.

The 1970s saw a dramatic deepening of ties between Japan and Indonesia in the area of the real economy, which was perhaps a sign that the establishment of Suharto's new order had finally produced what Japan had longed for over the years. Here was a unified and stable Indonesia that placed greater emphasis on the economy rather than on political ideology in its nation-building. As the absolute prerequisite for ensuring that this same trend spread throughout maritime Asia was stability in Indonesia, which was central to the region. We could say that this was the significance of Japan's efforts to consistently provide the largest amount of aid to this country.

In June 1970, just as the developmental policy of the Suharto regime was getting on track, news came of Sukarno's death at the age of 69. After his fall from power, Sukarno had refused to comply with the military's suggestion to flee the country and chose instead to remain in his homeland. But he faced a brutal fate. He was removed from the presidential palace and was soon stripped of the title of president and head of state. Not long after Suharto was formally appointed as the second president of the Republic of Indonesia in March 1968, Sukarno passed away amid isolation and hardship.

Had Sukarno sacrificed his principles to renounce the Communist Party and seek a compromise with the army following the September 30 Incident, he might have been able to remain in his post as president, even if it was only a symbolic role. Yet, at the end of his dramatic political career, Sukarno had refused to cave in, choosing instead to stick to his principles.

Furthermore, because he refused to flee and chose to die in misery in his homeland, Sukarno took on an aura of martyrdom. Indeed, it was for this reason that nearly thirty years later, when the Suharto regime was forced to the brink of collapse by the Asian financial crisis, the Indonesian people saw in Sukarno's daughter Megawati the likeness of her father, and in their enthusiasm elevated her to the position of president.

1965—the year that marked a turning point

We have been following the rivalry between countries over the future of Asian order, but rather than being a straightforward struggle for power, these rivalries arose out of the future vision of Asia held by each country. America pursued its ideal of Asia under Cold War circumstances primarily through the criteria of whether or not a country was Communist. Carried along by the tides of decolonization, the United Kingdom sought to construct an "unofficial empire" in its quest for a more moderate course. And vying with these two powers was China, which sought to lead Asia through Communism.

What place did Japan hold in this contest over the future direction of Asia, which pitted the Cold War (for the United States), decolonization (for the United Kingdom), and revolution (for China) against each other? Japan's postwar objective in Asia was above all to expand its own economic horizons. Yet, Japan was simultaneously motivated by its conviction that for Asia—divided as it was over the question of whether to take sides in the Cold War or lean toward revolution while reeling from military conflicts—the future lay not in political ideology, but in economic growth brought about by development. Underlying Japan's conviction was the idea that issues which might be construed as class conflict could in fact be resolved through economic growth—a worldview that had sustained Japan's own progress in the postwar era.

When we look back upon the trajectory of Japan's southward advance, we see how Japan moved to counter the effects of the Cold War and revolution— as well as attempts at moderating decolonization—by paying reparations to Indonesia as the United States intervened in its civil war, mediating in the Malaysian conflict over British objections, and engaging in a tug-of-war with China in the final stages of mediation. The major powers had become caught up in the contest in pursuit of their respective future visions of Asia precisely because they saw that the future of Asia depended on the direction taken by newly emerging countries that were gaining independence one after the other. In other words, it was a battle over decolonization.

Still, no matter how great the energy of decolonization was in shaping the contours of postwar Asia, it was predestined to end. The aspiration for independence can only exert its dynamic power to unite as long as the reality of colonial rule exists. By the end of the 1960s and early 1970s, colonialism in its intrinsic sense of territorial domination had disappeared from most parts of the world. And when the reality of colonial rule disappeared, the aspiration for independence was replaced by the new challenge of determining what to do with the independence that had been won.

But no matter how ardently Japan aspired toward development, it did not have the power to introduce the idea throughout Asia. Even Sukarno's Indonesia, to which Japan had devoted so much energy, chose to side with the Beijing–Jakarta Axis in the end. It is perhaps appropriate to see Japan as a player that was unable to set the scene in the same way as the United States, the United Kingdom, or China. Then again, none of these countries were successful in their attempts. Meanwhile, triggered in part by the completion of decolonization, the new tide of development began to spread far and wide across Asia. "From decolonization to development" was the principal trajectory followed by Asia in its postwar history, and it was formed by a dynamic that was inherent to Asia itself.

When we reflect on the enormous transformations that took place in Asia—from decolonization to development, from politics to economics— the year 1965 represented a turning point, or was, at any rate, the year that marked the beginning of such transformations.

In March 1965, America began sending its ground troops to Vietnam— increasing the roll call to 180,000 by the year's end and eventually to a maximum of 540,000—escalating the Vietnam War to an all-out conflict. Meanwhile, as we saw in the previous chapter, in June the coup d'état in Algeria led to the cancellation of the Second Asian-African Conference (Algiers Conference), while at the end of September, the September 30 Incident erupted in Indonesia, delivering a severe blow against the Beijing– Jakarta Axis overnight.

This series of developments highlight the significant setback suffered internationally by radical leftist groups, whose agenda included anti- colonialism and Communism. Since this was a favorable outcome for America, it gave rise to rumors of CIA involvement in the political up- heaval in both Algeria and Indonesia. It could be said that following the decline of forces championing anti-colonialism, Asia became a bipolarized region divided between Communist countries and those taking a pro-US, anti-Communist stance.[17]

However, there is perhaps a deeper meaning to the downfall of the leftists, in that it could have been an indication that independence and revolution had begun to diverge. More than anything else, Communism in postwar Asia had succeeded in establishing a powerful foothold by riding the wave of aspiration for independence from colonialism. But once independence had been achieved by advances in the tide of decolonization, the impetus for revolution inevitably lost its momentum as leaders like Sukarno, who personified the unity between independence and revolution, began to make their exit.

On the other hand, in Vietnam, where a full-blown war was raging, the strength that could only be derived by a combination of revolution and inde- pendence became painfully apparent to the United States and its Cold War logic. But even here, as the fall of Saigon was eventually followed by socialist nation-building that led to turmoil, revolution proved difficult to maintain once independence had been achieved.

In contrast, if we turn our gaze to Northeast Asia, the Treaty on Basic Relations between Japan and the Republic of Korea was signed in June 1965, normalizing relations between the two countries twenty years after World War II. The underlying factor was the US need to strengthen relation- ships between its Asian allies as it fought the Vietnam War; in that sense, this development was consistent with the logic of the Cold War.

At the same time, the signing of this treaty marked a milestone in South Korea's decolonization. Since its founding, decolonization for South Korea had been synonymous with eliminating Japan, and for this reason building its relationship with Japan presented a thorny issue that was directly linked to nationalism. The fierce anti-Japanese nationalism had come to the fore under the Rhee Syngman government, and the fact that the Park Chung-hee government pressed ahead with the normalization process—even as it faced vehement domestic opposition—had perhaps been an indication that South Korea's decolonization, which was closely linked to its relationship with Japan, had arrived at a turning point.

Viewing these developments from the Japanese standpoint, 1965 was a year in which both the scope and depth of its involvement in Asia expanded; this could be seen in its relationship with South Korea as well as with Indonesia, which was in the midst of its transition to the Suharto regime after the Beijing–Jakarta Axis was derailed. It is true that these were collaborative relationships with military regimes respectively led by Park Chung-hee and Suharto, who championed anti-Communism instead of independence, and in that sense they adhered to the Cold War structure. But at the same time, the considerable amount of economic aid extended by Japan served as a foothold for launching a "system of development" in both of these countries.

As the consummation of decolonization ended the honeymoon between independence and revolution, it seemed then that nation-building after achieving independence would be entrusted to development in combination with the logic of the Cold War. And the signs of change that emerged in 1965 became even more pronounced after the Cold War logic of the United States was defeated in Vietnam by an energy that was in all likelihood not that of revolution, but of independence.

However, any narrative of the change from politics to economics in postwar Asia must touch upon the outcome of the Cold War, which was the other principal influence in Asia; in other words, the dramatic thaw in relations between the United States and China known as the "Nixon Shock."

Notes

1 Dewi Sukarno, *Dewi Sukaruno jiden* [Autobiography of Dewi Sukarno] (Tokyo: Bungeishunju, 1978), 137.
2 "Mastermind testifies that 'Suharto was given prior notice' in the failed coup attempt of 1965," *Asahi Shimbun*, August 4, 1998.
3 Fumuhiko Kai, *Kokkyo wo koeta yujo: Waga gaiko hiwa* [Friendship across Borders: My Secret Stories of Diplomacy] (Tokyo: Tokyo Shimbun, 1990), 62–66.
4 "Aid for the Indonesian Army," Southeast Asia Division, October 7, 1965, Diplomatic Record of the Ministry of Foreign Affairs of Japan A'0211.
5 "Regarding the special meeting between President Sukarno and Japanese reporters," dispatch from Ambassador Saito to the Minister of Foreign Affairs, October 19, 1965, Diplomatic Record of the Ministry of Foreign Affairs of Japan A'0211.
6 Regarding the report to Prime Minister Sato, dispatch from Ambassador Saito, November 1, 1965, Diplomatic Record of the Ministry of Foreign Affairs of Japan A'0211.

7 "US diplomatic record. DOS to Djakarta, October 29, 1965," *FRUS, 1964–1968*, vol. 26.
 8 "Aid framework for stabilizing the Indonesian economy in response to new developments (Draft)," October 26, 1965, Diplomatic Record of the Ministry of Foreign Affairs of Japan A'0211.
 9 "Emergency aid for Indonesia," Asian Affairs Bureau, November 1, 1965, Diplomatic Record of the Ministry of Foreign Affairs of Japan A'0211.
10 "Emergency aid for Indonesia," Asian Affairs Bureau, November 26, 1965, Diplomatic Record of the Ministry of Foreign Affairs of Japan A'0211.
11 "Recent developments in Indonesia: Delegation of political authority to Armed Forces Commander Sukarno," Southeast Asian Division, March 15, 1965, Diplomatic Record of the Ministry of Foreign Affairs of Japan A'4-1-0-5-4.
12 "Policy on handling outstanding bilateral issues including economic cooperation relevant to the host nation of the Ministerial Conference for the Economic Development of Southeast Asia, Ministry of Foreign Affairs, April 4, 1966, Diplomatic Record of the Ministry of Foreign Affairs of Japan E'0054.
13 "Japanese policy on aid to Indonesia," Asian Affairs Bureau, April 26, 1966, Diplomatic Record of the Ministry of Foreign Affairs of Japan E'0054.
14 Ibid.
15 Ibid.
16 "Meeting of Indonesia's creditor nations: Summary of the joint communiqué," *Asahi Shimbun*, September 21, 1966.
17 Akira Suehiro, "Theory of Southeast Asian Economies," *Modern Japanese Society 3: International Comparisons (2)*, ed. Institute of Social Science (Tokyo: University of Tokyo Press, 1992), 288.

5 The thawing of the Asian Cold War

US–China rapprochement, and the emergence of the "China Issue"

Figure 5.1 Kakuei Tanaka (at right), newly elected president of the Liberal Democratic Party (LDP), and Foreign Minister Takeo Fukuda, who lost to Tanaka, congratulating one another after the election for the party presidency at the LDP convention, July 5, 1972, at the Prime Minister's Office.

Source: © Kyodo News.

China–US reconciliation: renunciation of revolution and the Cold War

"There is special news this afternoon—you are lost."[1] These were the very first words with which China's Premier Zhou Enlai greeted US National Security Advisor Henry Kissinger, who had deceived the entire world by secretly flying to Beijing after announcing he was taking a sick leave due to stomach problems during his visit to Pakistan. The meeting took place on July 9, 1971, and marked a historical moment when the United States and China shook hands for the first time since hostilities between the two countries began at the end of World War II.

Back in 1954, at the Geneva Conference, where settlement of the Korean War and the First Indochina War was discussed, US Secretary of State

Dulles had rejected Zhou's extended hand. Dulles's action was an expression of the stubborn US rejection of China, which had just made a dashing debut as a major Asian power at the conference. The moment had no doubt been an unforgettable humiliation for Zhou, who remained in charge of China's diplomacy for many years to follow; he referred to this incident repeatedly during his talk with Kissinger.

If one were to select the defining moments in international politics in postwar Asia, the US–China rapprochement staged by Richard Nixon, Henry Kissinger, Mao Zedong, and Zhou Enlai would probably count as one of the peak events, with the other being the fall of Saigon.

The rapprochement between the United States and China in the summer of 1971, together with the clandestine process through which it was accomplished, had a tremendous impact on the world. Because the US–China confrontation had been at the core of the Asian Cold War, it would not be too far-fetched to declare that this rapprochement marked the end of the Asian Cold War. (Agreement with this view might depend on whether one regards the subsequent USSR–US/Japan/China confrontation as an extension of the Asian Cold War.)

The US–China rapprochement, along with the dramatic diplomatic methods employed to engineer it, has often been regarded as a diplomatic masterpiece that transformed the triangular Cold War relationship of the United States, China, and the Soviet Union into one that pitted the United States and China against the Soviet Union. This view was particularly prevalent in Japan, where the shock of being "bypassed" by China and the United States remained fresh in the collective memory for a long time.

When placed in the context of the quest for order in postwar Asia—the principal topic of this book—what was the significance of this reconciliation between the two countries?

Simply put, the United States and China had struck a bargain. The United States, fatigued by the endless Vietnam War, gave up on its pursuit of the Cold War. China, unable to shoulder the weight of the task any longer, gave up on its quest for revolution according to its own purified ideology, for the sake of which the country had made an enemy of not only the United States but also the Soviet Union. A deal struck by two countries that had each given up its key policy—the Cold War on the part of the United States and revolution on the part of China—was the essential meaning of the US–China rapprochement.

At the center of the US Cold War strategy in Asia was its stubborn refusal to recognize the existence of Communist China. And it was not only a matter of confronting China; from the US perspective, "China" had to be represented by the nationalist government of Taiwan. The United States had intervened in Vietnam for fear of losing it to a domino-like spread of Communism in Asia. Yet, in spite of the 540,000 troops it had deployed in Vietnam, the situation became increasingly chaotic, exhausting even the resourceful United States.

Having succeeded President Johnson, who had stepped down totally bereft of measures for improving the situation in Vietnam, delivering the United States from the fiasco of the war was the top priority for the Nixon administration. And this was one of the ultimate goals behind Nixon and Kissinger's approach to China—that is, to seek China's help to escape from the quagmire in Vietnam, even though China had been the subject of US containment policy. To recognize Communist China in order to induce its cooperation was for the United States nothing short of abandoning its Cold War policy.

What about the Chinese side? Having pursued a policy of peaceful co-existence in the mid-1950s, China started to deepen its radical stance by the 1960s, intensifying its ideological dispute with the Soviet Union and restoring Mao Zedong's leadership. This was further strengthened with the launching of the Cultural Revolution in 1966. At one point, it al-most seemed possible for China to break out of the US containment and gain the upper hand in the dispute with the Soviet Union by forming the Beijing–Jakarta Axis with the increasingly left-leaning Indonesian pres-ident Sukarno, but that dream was dashed by Sukarno's downfall in the wake of the September 30 Incident.

Subsequently, while antagonistic relations with the United States contin-ued, China's confrontation with the Soviet Union intensified to the extent that by 1970, Mao and the Chinese leadership feared a full-scale Soviet mili-tary invasion. In order to deflect the massive pressure from the Soviet Union, the Chinese leadership decided to set about improving the country's rela-tions with the United States. For China—which had backed revolutionary forces in various regions in Asia while at the same time purifying its Com-munist ideology by criticizing the Soviets as "revisionists"—reconciliation with the United States meant a de facto renunciation of its policy of refining ideology and pursuing revolution.

This created an Asia in which the United States no longer waged its Cold War and China no longer pursued its revolution. It also coincided with the disappearance of regional leaders such as Indonesia's Sukarno, whose life-long mission had been independence, and of the colonial powers, including Britain, which had given rise to such "heroes" of independence. In a nut-shell, grand politics centered on such lofty ideas as the Cold War, revolution, and independence had perished from Asia. And it was the disappearance of such grand politics, which could divide a nation's future into two paths, that provided the political foundation for the era of development that spread throughout Asia after the 1970s.

Japan's sudden rapprochement with China

On the flip side, the demise of grand politics also meant that countries in Asia were liberated from the ideological restraints that had been imposed on them. Having witnessed the thawing of the Cold War between China and the United States, countries in the region began to move at once to secure a desirable position for themselves in the new international environment. Suddenly, the situation in Asia became highly fluid. The era of grand politics was one in which countries struggled for power on the merits of their respective ideologies, and now that it had ended, Asia was given the impetus to resume its game of balance, effectively embracing the classical dynamics of international politics.

Faced with this situation, Japan reacted most vehemently. The US-China rapprochement had taken place behind its back, and the frequency with which the Japanese media referred to the "Nixon shock" was an indication of just how gravely Japan had been affected by the event.

But the shock experienced by the Japanese represented only half of the picture. In fact, Japan's almost instantaneous rush to normalize diplomatic relations with China, as if to avenge Washington's unilateral action, had similarly far-reaching repercussions in the international politics of the Asia-Pacific region. This fact tends to be neglected in Japan because it was overshadowed by the "Nixon shock."

Actually, besides the initial shock, the rapprochement had given rise to a certain sense of expectation among leaders of the Japanese government, including the Foreign Ministry. Now that Japan was relieved from the constraints of the US-China Cold War, it was presented with the opportunity to pursue an open approach to normalizing diplomatic relations with China. Around that time, Prime Minister Eisaku Sato was expected to triumphantly step down after having accomplished the return of Okinawa to Japan in May 1972. There was a fierce race to succeed Sato between Ministry of International Trade and Industry (MITI) Minister Kakuei Tanaka and Foreign Minister Takeo Fukuda. Although Fukuda was Sato's personal choice, Masayoshi Ohira and Takeo Miki, who were also serious contenders, endorsed Tanaka on the condition that closer ties with China would be promoted. Consequently, Tanaka was elected president of the LDP. As prime minister, Tanaka visited Beijing in September soon after he formed his cabinet, and in one grand gesture, normalized diplomatic relations with China. Japan was subsequently overtaken by what could be described as a "China boom."

We should recall that the Shanghai Communiqué adopted in February 1972 when President Nixon visited Beijing was nothing but a parallel enumeration of the American and Chinese positions; it took another seven years before diplomatic relations were normalized. In comparison, Japan moved with astonishing speed to achieve reconciliation and normalization of diplomatic relations in one go. This was, of course, an expression of Japan's desire to reconcile with China—a desire that had long been suppressed by the United States. It seems undeniable that Japan's action stemmed also from the psychology—to which not a small number on the Japanese side have confessed—on the part of Japan to get back at Washington by normalizing diplomatic relations with China ahead of the United States.

While the above developments are remembered in Japan solely as a sequence of events starting with the "Nixon shock," followed by the normalization of diplomatic ties with China and the subsequent "China boom," they take on a completely different meaning when placed in the wider context of international politics in Asia.

Officially, the Nixon administration expressed no particular objections to Japan's normalization of diplomatic ties with China. However, the true reaction in Washington had not been so simple, as evidenced by recently disclosed information in which Kissinger refers to Japan as "the worst traitor." In seeking to normalize its relations with China, Japan severed its diplomatic ties with Taiwan. On its part, the United States had taken great pains to build its relationship with China while sustaining its relations with Taiwan at the same. Since Japan's actions made this task that much more difficult, some say the Nixon administration was quite displeased by the decision made by the Tanaka government.

The impact of Japan's prompt reconciliation with China was also significant for other Asia-Pacific countries. Since Japan was the dominant power among the pro-Western countries in the region, it was only natural that its actions would have serious repercussions.

Indonesia, a pivotal country for Japan's reentry to Southeast Asia, responded to Japan's moves with a grave sense of crisis. Retracing the complex actions taken by President Suharto at this time will reveal the impact that Japan's rapid reconciliation with China had on the Asia-Pacific region.

Suharto's enigmatic visit to Japan

President Suharto visited Japan on May 9, 1972. It was his third visit to Japan since assuming the presidency, which he had snatched away from Sukarno. Suharto's visit at this time puzzled people in both Japan and Indonesia, because the Japanese side had not yet reciprocated his previous visits by paying a courtesy call, and there was no matter of urgent concern between the two countries. Most of all, the return of Okinawa, which was expected to be the farewell accomplishment of the Eisaku Sato cabinet, was supposed to take place toward the end of that month, and competition between Takeo Fukuda and Kakuei Tanaka, the two chief contenders for the presidency of the governing LDP (and thus the prime ministership) after Sato, was heating up. As such, under normal conditions, it would hardly have been considered an appropriate timing for a foreign dignitary to visit Japan, particularly because he would not know whom to meet among Japanese government leaders.

Suharto bowed out of official ceremonies, such as a courtesy visit to the imperial palace, and instead focused on meeting with leaders of the Japanese government and the LDP. Behind this enigmatic trip was Suharto's sense of urgency stemming from Japan's sudden approach toward China.

As pointed out earlier, Suharto had taken control of the military as a result of the September 30 Incident, established domestic stability by ousting the Communist Party, and emerged victorious from the power struggle with Sukarno. For Suharto, who claimed to have saved the country by crippling the subversive schemes of the Communist Party and its behind-the-scenes patron, China, anti-Communism was the very core of his government's legitimacy.

Thus, Suharto viewed China as the most dangerous presence, whose actions called for utmost vigilance. It is indeed an established fact that even after Suharto seized power, China continued its attempts to intervene in Indonesian politics through the country's ethnic Chinese who were affiliated with the former Communist Party. For instance, China maintained activities to facilitate Sukarno's comeback and initiated riots in various locations so that Suharto's ability to bring situations under control would be called into question. The greatest threat from China was its influence over the ethnic Chinese population in Indonesia, which led to domestic issues that were deeply rooted in the country's politics. As such, the threat China posed to Suharto's Indonesia was of a different nature from conventional international issues.

In Suharto's view, the US–China rapprochement had no bearing on the threat from China. As emphasized in the Shanghai Communiqué adopted at the time of Nixon's visit to China, "The Chinese side stated that it firmly supports the struggles of all oppressed people and nations for freedom and liberation." China had declared its intention to continue the liberation struggle, which, far from being rhetoric represented a real menace for Indonesia.

And now, even as China remained a threat to Indonesia, Japan had followed the US lead in a headlong rush to normalize its diplomatic ties with China. Both the United States and Japan were overseas supporters of the Suharto government, so this move by Japan was of serious concern to Suharto. The sole motivation behind what appeared to be an abrupt visit was his wish to somehow put the brakes on this undesirable trend.

While the general purpose of his visit was to stem Japan's advances toward China by convincing leaders of the Japanese government and the LDP of the threat posed by Communist China, Suharto had a more concrete wish of seeing Takeo Fukuda elected as the new president of the LDP. Fukuda was known to be more cautious about relations with China than Tanaka, his major contender. But that was not the only reason Suharto wished Fukuda to lead the Japanese government. As a senior member of the Indonesian government once said, "Fukuda is well known by a number of Indonesians, while Tanaka is not." Well-developed relations existed between Fukuda and Indonesia.

As discussed in Chapter 2, civil war broke out in Indonesia toward the end of the 1950s, and anti-Communist rebels had at one point succeeded in establishing a provisional government, which was subsequently suppressed by Sukarno, forcing the rebels to flee the country. Fukuda had offered protection and assistance to these rebel leaders and had maintained longstanding relations with Indonesians on the anti-Communist side. Fukuda had also been instrumental in collating various views within Japan to organize the meeting of Indonesia's creditor nations and subsequent mechanisms of support. It would not be an overstatement to say that in Japan, Fukuda was the central supporter of the Suharto regime.

In contrast, Tanaka was not only unknown in Indonesia, but was backed by Masayoshi Ohira and Takeo Miki, who both supported rapprochement, and it was believed that a rapid rapprochement between Japan and China would inevitably follow if Tanaka were elected as LDP president.

Aside from being deeply wary of China politically, the Indonesian side was equally, if not more, concerned about the possibility that further improvement in China–Japan relations might divert aid and investment from Japan away from Indonesia to the Chinese continent.

As for the United States, the Nixon administration, having grown weary of the heavy burden imposed by the Vietnam War, had announced its intention to "localize" the war in Vietnam, reduce its burden, and request its allies to reinforce their respective self-defence efforts. It was with this rationale that the United States informed the Indonesian government that it would downscale its aid to Indonesia. It was imperative, therefore, for Suharto to prevent the diversion of Japan's economic aid to China now that the US aid was to be reduced.

Having asked himself whether Indonesia had enough bargaining power to block Japan's approach to China, Suharto concluded that he would have to improvise. He put forth a diplomatic proposal for a "Japan–Australia–Indonesia trilateral cooperative scheme" and sought to contribute to Fukuda's election as LDP president by manipulating vested interests between Japan and Indonesia.

The Japan–Australia–Indonesia trilateral cooperative scheme

One of the measures that Suharto conceived to limit Japan's rapprochement with China was a cooperative framework among Japan, Indonesia, and Australia. Australia was believed to share a common interest with Indonesia in keeping Japan away from China. Suharto hoped that such a cooperative framework would work to restrain Japan.

Behind this scheme was Suharto's analysis of the situation as follows: The threat from China remained the same even after the US–China rapprochement; the United States, overburdened as it was by the Vietnam War, was leaning more strongly toward withdrawal from Asia. Meanwhile, the United Kingdom, which had played a central role in the security of maritime Asia together with the United States, had withdrawn from Singapore. Consequently, the only viable counterweight against China would be Japan. Suharto believed that Australia also shared this view; in Suharto's mind, Indonesia and Australia were in a similar situation. It made sense for Indonesia to pursue a Tokyo–Jakarta–Canberra Axis in place of the Beijing–Jakarta Axis that had been proposed toward the end of the Sukarno era.

Prior to Suharto's visit to Japan, the governor of the Bank Indonesia arrived in Tokyo to pave the way for the arrival of the Indonesian president. It is believed that Fukuda endorsed the proposed tripartite scheme in his talk with the visiting central banker. Taking into consideration Fukuda's long and deep association with Indonesia, as well as his advocacy for a more cautious approach to normalizing diplomatic ties with China based on maintaining a proper balance of relations with other countries, such an endorsement by Fukuda does not seem entirely implausible.

President Suharto visited Japan in May 1972. He met with a succession of Japanese government leaders starting with Prime Minister Sato, Foreign Minister Fukuda, and MITI Minister Tanaka. As it turned out, however, Suharto proposed his "tripartite scheme" only in very vague terms.

In his first meeting with Prime Minister Sato, Suharto limited himself to pointing out that

> Japanese cooperation with Southeast Asian countries on the one hand, and Australia and New Zealand on the other, would contribute to a reduction of the international tensions in Asia caused by the superpowers, even in the absence of a formal, binding treaty.[2]

In response, Sato expressed his view—which was completely counter to Suharto's intentions—saying that "an improvement in Sino-Japanese relations would also be beneficial to peace in Asia."[3] When Suharto stressed the danger of China's subversive and invasive intentions during talks with Japanese government leaders, some on the Japanese side interpreted his comments as an attempt to legitimatize his military rule in Indonesia. Thus, there existed a wide gap in perception between the two governments.

In contrast to his subdued approach toward his own "tripartite scheme," Suharto was very energetic in securing economic aid and investment from Japan during his visit. For instance, Suharto requested Japan's investment in a large-scale development project on the island of Sumatra and asked for an expansion of Japan's economic aid beyond the share stipulated by the Inter-Governmental Group on Indonesia (IGGI). It had been decided by the IGGI, which had met several times since its inception, that Japan, the United States, and the Western European countries including France, Germany, and the Netherlands should each contribute a third of Indonesia's overall financing. Suharto was asking Japan to provide financial aid beyond this one-third share. Moreover, he also requested a new yen loan for oil development separate from the IGGI framework.

When soliciting Japan's assistance for these projects, Suharto was very specific and tenacious, quoting detailed figures. While Foreign Minister Fukuda made only subtle, sardonic remarks, saying, "I find His Excellency is not only the republic's president but also the finance minister and the national development minister," MITI Minister Tanaka was much more straightforward, declaring that such details were not appropriate for ministerial level talks, at which Suharto was openly embarrassed. Agreement on the provision of the new yen loan that Suharto sought was finally reached after tough negotiations, during which the Japanese side definitely felt uncomfortable with Suharto's negotiation style. Tanaka in particular did not hide his displeasure. Because Tanaka's view on policy toward China was believed to be fundamentally different from that of Suharto, the general sense arose that if Tanaka were to succeed Sato as prime minister of Japan, Indonesia's relations with Japan would become difficult.

Even though Suharto only vaguely proposed the tripartite scheme involving Japan, Australia, and Indonesia, Japanese officials had grasped the intention behind it through various channels. On the basis of the information they had gathered, they judged it best to postpone a decision on the scheme until the situation in the region, which had become fluid due to the US–China rapprochement, became clearer. In concrete terms, this meant Japan would wait and see what would become of the Asian Pacific Council (ASPAC) and ASEAN.

ASPAC was a regional organization founded in 1966 following a proposal by Korean president Park Chung-hee. Its members included Japan, Australia, South Korea, New Zealand, the Philippines, Thailand, Malaysia, South Vietnam, and Taiwan. ASPAC aimed to strengthen relations among participating countries through various activities, including the annual ministerial conference.

Park Chung-hee clearly intended ASPAC to strengthen solidarity among anti-Communist countries in Asia and render support to such frontline anti-Communist regimes as South Korea and South Vietnam. Some countries in the region, including Japan, did not appreciate the organization's anti-Communist bias. Nevertheless, for countries like Japan and Australia, ASPAC was the only forum that allowed multilateral discussion of political issues in Asia. As such, Japan had to give due attention to this organization, even though its unifying power was weak from the beginning.

Antagonism between the United States and China had provided the basic structure of the Cold War in Asia, and as tensions began to ease, the *raison d'être* of ASPAC came under question. Japan looked on with interest to discern the future course of this organization, but no more ministerial conferences were held after June 1973. Subsequently, ASPAC quietly expired.

The other regional organization that Japan paid close attention to was ASEAN, which was founded in 1967. At the time of Suharto's visit, the Japanese government felt this organization was "still struggling to define its role and future course of action."[4] ASEAN was in the midst of discussions regarding a "Southeast Asia neutralization scheme" proposed by Malaysia, which was aimed at creating a neutralized Southeast Asia with the agreement of superpowers outside the region, including the United States, China, and the Soviet Union. It was an attempt to deal with changes in the international environment caused by the gradual withdrawal of the United States and the United Kingdom from Asia on the one hand, and the expansion of the Chinese and Soviet presence in Asia on the other. The Soviet idea of collective security in Asia proposed in 1969, and China's bid to obtain a seat at the United Nations in 1971, both exemplify their growing presence in Asia at the time.

Indonesia, which saw itself as *the* core member of ASEAN, however, remained lukewarm toward this neutralization scheme. Given its history of suffering at the hands of foreign powers, which began with the independence war with the Netherlands and continued with the US intervention in its civil war and the alleged foreign involvement in the September 30 Incident, Indonesia remained strongly suspicious of this idea of securing with the "guarantee of outside superpowers."

The ASEAN Foreign Minister Conference in November 1971 only went as far as to confirm that neutralization was a desirable goal, leaving the direction of ASEAN's security scheme undecided. The framework of ASEAN itself remained quite fluid, as was made clear by Philippine Foreign Minister Carlos P. Romulo's suggestion that Australia and New Zealand be invited to join the organization as members.

Given these circumstances, the Japanese government judged it best to postpone its deliberation on the proposed Japan–Australia–Indonesia trilateral cooperation until the future directions of ASPAC and ASEAN were confirmed. The decision was based on its view that the still uncertain future of ASPAC and ASEAN depended on the shifting balance among superpowers in Asia triggered by the US-China rapprochement, and as such, "the future direction of these organizations would become clear only when countries in the region adjusted their respective relations with China." The Japanese government judged that until then, it should further consolidate bilateral relations with countries in the region.

Also, the Japanese side was suspicious of the "trilateral" framework of cooperation itself. Japan feared that Indonesia would benefit by bringing all its contending issues into the trilateral relations, while Japan would gain nothing from Indonesia's involvement in its bilateral relationship with Australia. Japan also had to take into consideration the reactions of other Southeast Asian countries should it enter into a special relationship with Indonesia. Moreover, there were undeniably anti-Chinese implications to the proposed trilateral cooperation scheme that could further narrow Japan's policy options at a time when adjustments to its policies on China seemed inevitable once Prime Minister Sato stepped down. In a nutshell, it appeared to Japan's leaders that the proposed trilateral cooperation would greatly benefit Indonesia, while offering next to nothing for Japan.

The election of Kakuei Tanaka and the termination of concessions

While Indonesia's tripartite scheme evoked only lukewarm reaction from the Japanese side, it was merely one part of Indonesia's approach.

There was speculation at the time that the direction of Japan's relationship with China would depend on the result of the coming LDP presidential election to determine Sato's successor. If Tanaka won, pro-rapprochement forces would prevail; if Fukuda won, a more cautious approach to China would be adopted. Realizing this, Indonesia tried another behind-the-scenes tactic in addition to proposing the trilateral cooperation scheme, in which it sought to align Indonesia's interests with various LDP factions to support Fukuda's victory in the election.

The following account relies on declassified Australian diplomatic documents; most of them, however, are actually primary source materials provided by the Japanese government, including the Foreign Ministry, as well as by those in Japanese political circles. Since Australia had also been approached by Indonesia about its tripartite scheme, the Australian government had assiduously collected information on Indonesian moves toward Japan. Quotes in the following section are taken from these Australian diplomatic documents.

As a Japanese Foreign Ministry official grumbled, "Japan's relations with Indonesia have been so closely intertwined with Japan's domestic politics that its decisions on Indonesia are often decided outside the Ministry of Foreign Affairs." Ever since the days of the Sukarno government, Japan's dealings with Indonesia were marked by a conspicuous tendency of being carried out through non-diplomatic channels, at the behest of such central figures in Japanese politics as Nobusuke Kishi and Hayato Ikeda.

Meanwhile, some Japanese diplomats spoke of special arrangements in Japan-Indonesia trade, whereby some of the commissions derived from the transactions were diverted to certain factions within the LDP. In return for these commissions, the Indonesian side expected special benefits. It is believed that a similar arrangement also existed in Japan's trade with the Philippines. Incidentally, suspicion of shady deals related to the war reparations and economic aid surfaced in Japan when the Marcos dictatorship fell in 1986; these allegations (the "Marcos Scandals") later became the subject of extensive parliamentary investigations.

During his visit to Japan in 1972, Suharto sought to promote the election of Fukuda with the aim of blocking a further deepening in Japan's relationship with China. Of all the possible means of influencing an LDP presidential election, Suharto chose the direct approach of offering support for concessions—or, more bluntly, channeling funds. As one observer put it, "Suharto's primary interest during the visit lay in promoting the Sato–Fukuda line...He succeeded [in doing so] to a certain extent because, after his visit, commissions related to oil trade began to flow to the Fukuda faction."

In those days, Takeo Kimura, a member of the House of Representatives, was the central figure in the so-called "Indonesia lobby" in Japanese political circles. Although Kimura belonged to the Sato faction, he was personally close to Fukuda, with whom he shared common interests related to economic aid and investments in Indonesia. Nevertheless, when the candidates for Sato's successor were narrowed down to Fukuda and Tanaka, Kimura threw his active support behind Tanaka.

Kimura also made a decisive effort to obtain a new yen loan for oil development from the Japanese government after negotiations on the matter ran into rough waters. One of his aims was to secure the "spoils" of his efforts for the Tanaka faction in the form of commissions. But Prime Minister Sato allegedly influenced the arrangements so that the commissions would flow to the Fukuda faction instead. Strongly displeased by this incident, the Tanaka faction later took revenge after forming the cabinet, as we shall see below.

Given the uncertainty regarding Prime Minister Sato's successor and the scheduled visit by US vice president Spiro Agnew to attend the ceremony for the return of Okinawa to Japan, Suharto's visit "came at the worst possible timing from a political viewpoint." But it had been calculated to bolster his hidden agenda. As noted by observers, "factions within the LDP were running up a tremendous amount of expenses for the closely-fought LDP presidential election, and they all needed to fill their empty coffers." Therefore, "the Indonesian side judged that it would be able to strike a good bargain with the Japanese if Suharto visited Japan at this particular time." And "for this reason, Suharto's visit to Japan was scheduled to occur before the LDP presidential election."

However, the election ended with Tanaka's victory, in a stunning turn of events for the Indonesian side, which had hoped for and anticipated Fukuda's election. Thus, in August 1972, immediately after Tanaka formed his cabinet, Suharto dispatched his special envoy Sudjono Humardani to Tokyo. An ex-military man, Humardani was Suharto's closest confidant in charge of financial matters, and was later labeled "Indonesia's Rasputin." He handled the financial matters related to Indonesia's relationship with Japan and had traveled frequently between the two countries.

Although it was assumed that a basic agreement had been reached between the two countries on the new yen loan for oil development, which Suharto had sought during his May 1972 visit, Japan had placed the administrative procedures for the loan on hold.

When Humardani visited in August, the Japanese side declared that informal channels could no longer be relied on for bilateral relations following the formation of the Tanaka cabinet. Humardani, they said, was therefore not authorized to negotiate on this matter. In the end, the agreement on the new loan was finally signed in October, but the Japanese strongly reiterated that future provision of the loan was to be strictly handled through official channels.

As we saw earlier, thanks to Indonesia's support for Fukuda's election and Sato's maneuvering, the commissions generated by this proposed oil project had been directed toward the Fukuda faction at the time of the LDP presidential election. Taken on its own, eliminating the powerful informal channels that existed between Japan and Indonesia and insisting on conducting bilateral relations through official channels was a legitimate argument. However, in view of the circumstances, the elimination of informal channels and the concurrent suspension of loan provision procedures could be interpreted as an attempt by the victorious Tanaka faction to shut down the vested interests of the Fukuda faction.

Humardani, on his part, explained to Tanaka that Suharto preferred to use his close associates to conduct transactions informally rather than relying on formal diplomatic channels. This information eventually succeeded in persuading Tanaka to retain the informal channel with Indonesia through Humardani.

While stressing the virtues of the informal channel, Humardani also emphasized the threat of Communist China. He informed Tanaka that Suharto, who had been obsessed with the fear of China since the September 30 Incident, was convinced that China would seize every opportunity to topple the Japanese government. This indicates that, even after the formation of the Tanaka cabinet, Suharto had not given up on preaching the dangers of rapprochement with China to Japan.

Tanaka responded by explaining that the normalization of diplomatic ties with China was significant for Japan as a means to recompense the Chinese people for Japan's misdeeds in the 1930s and 1940s, build long-term trade relations, and establish a new balance of power among the superpowers. In fact, a month after he met with Humardani, Prime Minister Tanaka flew to Beijing and restored Japan's diplomatic relations with China in a single stroke.

While seeking to mend its relationship with Tanaka, the Indonesian side decided to target Yasuhiro Nakasone, who became MITI Minister in the Tanaka cabinet, to succeed Takeo Kimura as the next collaborator with Indonesia. When Humardani revisited Japan in early October 1972, he met Nakasone to seek his cooperation, to which Nakasone is said to have consented.

From the Indonesian viewpoint, Nakasone was a prominent contender in the future succession race to Prime Minister Tanaka; for its part, the Nakasone side valued the staunch anti-Communist stance of the Suharto government. Subsequently, senior legislators of the Nakasone faction visited Indonesia with senior MITI officials and "consulted" with government leaders and officials of development-related government bureaus. The records show that neither Prime Minister Tanaka nor other LDP leaders were informed of these consultations.

The "China Issue" surfaces

In the end, it is clear that Suharto's bid to block Japan's rapid rapprochement with China had failed, despite his efforts to involve Australia and to influence the rivalries between LDP factions. At the time, there was tremendous pressure within Japan for normalizing diplomatic relations with China, which was to gain a runaway momentum that ultimately pushed Tanaka, instead of Fukuda, to the top position.

In the face of such a gigantic force, Suharto and Indonesia were simply powerless. Needless to say, Suharto was well aware of the situation, and that was precisely why he proposed the "Japan–Australia–Indonesia" cooperation scheme. Yet, in the final analysis, we must agree with the accuracy of the Australian Foreign Ministry's assessment, that "It was a miscalculation on the part of Indonesia to expect that it could influence Japan's China policy."

If Indonesia had indeed been powerless against the domestic forces that drive Japan, Suharto's attempt would have been no more than an episode of the times. However, when we turn our attention from our evaluation of his proposed framework and look beyond, we will see how Suharto's complex maneuvers at the time had heralded the arrival of a new era in Asia—an era that was to be characterized by the emergence of the "China issue."

One of the most difficult issues faced by Asian countries in the postwar era was defining the nature of their respective relationship with Communist China, which had emerged after World War II. India's Nehru sought a way to peacefully coexist with this giant in the north by upholding the Five Principles of Peaceful Coexistence, while Sukarno's downfall began with the Beijing–Jakarta Axis and ended with the September 30 Incident.

However, as long as the United States refused to recognize Communist China and pursued its policy of containment, deciding how to relate with China was an issue that many Asian countries, including Japan, did not have to address, at least in realistic terms. This all changed after the dramatic thawing of the Cold War between the United States and China, which forced each country to face up to the new—and yet old—question of maintaining a proper distance with respect to China, a gigantic presence at the heart of Asia.

Motivated by his mounting fear that Japan, inspired by the US–China rapprochement, might rush to improve its relations with China, Suharto made a frantic effort—even going as far as to involve Australia—to block Japan's path. Suharto's actions were an indication that the lifting of the "partition" imposed by the US–China Cold War had opened the way to a new era of alliance building in Asia.

Japan's China policy: two views

Japan's response to Suharto's proposal for a tripartite scheme revealed the existence of two schools of thought within Japan regarding the "China issue." The Tanaka school placed utmost priority on promoting relations with China, whereas the Fukuda school advocated a more cautious approach that included maintaining a proper balance in Japan's relations with other neighboring countries.

The Tanaka school, marked by its predominant interest in China, tended to overlook Southeast Asia as it remained in the shadows. Meanwhile, the Fukuda school placed greater emphasis on Southeast Asia as an important counterbalance against China. The clear contrast in their response to the tripartite scheme, between Tanaka's indifference and Fukuda's active interest, vividly illustrated the respective priorities in their thinking.

Later, when Prime Minister Tanaka toured Southeast Asia in January 1974, he was met by fierce anti-Japan riots in Thailand and Indonesia. In Jakarta, Tanaka was surrounded by violent demonstrators and had to be evacuated by helicopter. While it is said that the riots were mainly caused by domestic power struggles, the slogans witnessed at these anti-Japan demonstrations included such criticisms as "Prime Minister Tanaka must modify his exclusively pro-Beijing diplomatic stance" and "The September 30 Incident was initiated by Beijing, PKI (Communist Party of Indonesia), and pro-Communist ethnic Chinese," along with more economic arguments, such as "Japanese companies should end their exclusive reliance on overseas Chinese" and "Japanese companies should choose *pribumi* [native Indonesian companies] as partners."

Only three years later, in 1977, Fukuda also visited Southeast Asia after becoming prime minister. During his visit, he announced what later came to be known as the Fukuda Doctrine. It advocated relationships based on "heart-to-heart mutual trust" and Japan's role as a bridge between ASEAN and other countries in Indochina. The warm welcome with which the Southeast Asian countries received the doctrine was beyond initial expectations.

The stark difference with the rough welcome given to Tanaka was no coincidence. In Fukuda's emphasis on omnidirectional peace diplomacy, we can see his intention of simultaneously pursuing improved relations with the Soviet Union and other countries so as to create a balance with Japan's signing of the Treaty of Peace and Friendship with the People's Republic of China.[5]

Although the two trends of thought on the China issue were to underpin Japanese diplomacy in the years that followed the US–China rapprochement, they remained obscured by the US–Japan–China "pseudo-alliance" against the Soviet Union during the height of the neo-Cold War in the 1980s. But the collapse of the Soviet Union brought with it an era of continuous political friction between Japan and China, despite the growing economic ties enjoyed by the two countries. Prompted by this changing relationship, the two trends are perhaps showing signs of a resurgence.

The history of Japan's postwar diplomacy has been studied predominantly in terms of its core relationship with the United States, as evidenced by the frequently-cited dichotomy of seeking either "self-determination" or "cooperation." However, it may be that as its relationship with the United States grows in intensity and stability, Japan is being left with an ever-smaller margin of choice with regard to how it relates to the United States. If the "China issue" were to replace that core relationship and the manner in which Japan relates to China should become the dividing line for Japanese diplomacy, the two underlying trends in Japan's policy toward China may gain in importance in the years to come.

Zhou Enlai's lamentation

Zhou Enlai passed away in Beijing on January 8, 1976. Already suffering from cancer at the time, Zhou had poured the last of his strengths into the momentous task of achieving a rapprochement with the United States and subsequently normalizing diplomatic relations with Japan. His last days were filled with a series of hardships. It has been said that Zhou's greatest wish at that point was to avoid being ousted toward the end of his life, for that would be tantamount to a complete negation of his lifetime devotion to revolution. For this reason, Zhou had to subjugate himself to Mao and make a substantial commitment to the Cultural Revolution, which he had not wholeheartedly supported.

In September 1971, Lin Biao, who was believed to have masterminded a botched coup against Mao, was killed when his plane crashed in Mongolia on his escape from China. A Communist Party functionary happened to witness Zhou lamenting the turn of events alone in his office. The bewildered functionary describes the encounter as follows:

> "Lin Biao has self-destructed," I noted, "so we should feel better because from now on the nation can focus on the task of developing the economy." Zhou was obviously touched by such comments because tears welled up in his eyes and streamed silently down his face and he began to cry louder and louder. He became so choked up at one point that he couldn't speak. Li Xiannian and I saw him crying so badly that we didn't know what to say, and so we just stood there to keep him company. In the end, the premier gradually calmed down, and after a long pause he uttered those few words: "You don't understand. It's not that simple. It's not finished." With that he said not one more word.[6]

Speculating as to why Premier Zhou Enlai was lamenting, the same functionary said:

> [T]he root of Zhou's sorrow was buried in the profound differences between his and Mao's ideas for managing the country. Mao wanted perpetual class struggle and endless political campaigns, but Zhou wanted to develop the economy. With Lin Biao out of the picture, the question for China was whose view of the country's future would win out as both leaders approached their final days.[7]

Whenever Japan sought to engage with Asia, regardless of the context, Japan had found itself confronted by the formidable presence of Zhou Enlai. From his dashing debut at the Bandung Conference and the tug-of-war over Sukarno's Indonesia to the US–China rapprochement and normalization of diplomatic ties with Japan, Zhou had made his presence known.

The lamentation of the great statesman may conversely shed light on the course taken by postwar Japan. In the end, Communist China under the leadership of Mao and Zhou never succeeded in bringing affluence to the Chinese people. The remorse for this failure might have been behind Zhou's lamentation.

In contrast, affluence was the greatest accomplishment of postwar Japan. What, then, had Japan failed to achieve—or, rather, chosen not to pursue— that post-revolution China had accomplished under Mao and Zhou? We could say that it was independence. China had pursued the path of "self-reliance"—even, occasionally, at the expense of the day-to-day lives of its people. And throughout this pursuit, it had maintained a strong will to remain an independent presence in the international community. Postwar Japan, in contrast, had chosen to pursue affluence under the "nuclear-and-US-dollar umbrella" of the United States.[8]

The contrasting paths taken by China and Japan in the postwar period had perhaps been a reflection of the different course each had taken in their past. It is only natural that the main goal for the newly born Communist China was to liberate itself from the dependent—and at times described as semi-colonial—position it had found itself in since its defeat in the First Opium War. The Korean War was the first war in which China was evenly matched with the Western powers since the Opium War. Shigeru Yoshida reportedly described the Chinese Army at the time as a motley mob of coolies that offered no cause for alarm. That was precisely how China had been perceived before World War II.

In contrast, imperial Japan, which had boasted of an outstanding position in Asia as one of the five world powers and as one of the world's three naval powers, lost everything in a grand war it fought against most of the world. One could say that after World War II, Japan made its own choice to step down from the arena of international power politics.

Even today, under circumstances that are drastically different from the past, the politics of independence and affluence may lie hidden as the two countries pursue their future course and as Asia seeks to establish regional order.

Faced with Zhou Enlai's death, Mao Zedong maintained an aloof posture. Mao had been obsessed with the fear that if Zhou outlived him, he would renounce the Cultural Revolution and start acting like the Soviet Union's Nikita Khrushchev, who denounced Stalin after the dictator's death. Some even believed that this fear made Mao deliberately delay Zhou's treatment for cancer.[9] As it turned out, however, Mao outlived Zhou for only eight months.

Meanwhile, spontaneous actions by people mourning Zhou Enlai triggered the First Tiananmen Incident in 1976. Deng Xiaoping was held

responsible for the incident and purged for the second time, only to be reha-
bilitated soon after Mao's death. After his second comeback, Deng took the
helm of the government in place of Hua Guofeng and steered the country
toward economic reform under the slogan of "reform and opening up."

The US–China rapprochement cast off the yoke of the Asian Cold War and
instantly raised the volatility of international politics in Asia. Nevertheless,
it fell short of changing the course of the major current of the times—the
shift from decolonization to development. In fact, by incorporating China,
which was about to embrace a policy of "reform and opening up" under
Deng Xiaoping, the current gained further momentum as an irreversible
force as it spread to all corners of Asia.

Notes

1 "Memorandum of Conversation, July 9, 1971," *FRUS, 1969–1972*, vol. 27.
2 "Minutes of the Meeting between Prime Minister Sato and President Suharto of
   Indonesia (First Session)," May 10, 1972. Documents released by the Ministry of
   Foreign Affairs of Japan, Information Disclosure No. 2005-00324.
3 Ibid.
4 Tokyo to Department of Foreign Affairs, Australia, June 6, 1972. The National
   Archives of Australia, A1838 3034/11/89 Part 10.
5 Hidekazu Wakatsuki, *"Zen-hoi gaiko" no jidai: Reisen hen'yo-ki no Nippon to
   Ajia—1971–80* [The Era of "Omnidirectional Diplomacy": Japan and Asia in
   the Transformative Period of the Cold War—1971–80] (Tokyo: Nihon Keizai
   Hyouronsha, 2006), Chapter 3.
6 Gao Wenqian, *Zhou Enlai: The Last Perfect Revolutionary* (New York: Public
   Affairs, 2008), 227.
7 Ibid.
8 Osamu Ishii, "Nichibei paatonaashippu e no dotei" [Road to the US-Japan part-
   nership], *Nichibei kankei tsushi* [A Comprehensive History of Japan-US Rela-
   tions], ed. Chihiro Hosoya (Tokyo: University of Tokyo Press, 1995).
9 Wenqian, *Zhou Enlai*, 95.

Epilogue

The depoliticization of Asia and postwar Japan

Struck by the "Western impact" and swallowed by it, Asia was placed under colonial rule by Western countries for several centuries. Yet, while colonial rule had seemed robust enough to last forever, it buckled all too easily under the "Eastern impact" of an invasion by Imperial Japan once World War II broke out. And in the aftermath of a war that saw a brief period of occupation by Japan and the demise of its empire, history began its resounding advance in Asia. The main melody that rang out was powered by the energy emanating from the desire to break free from colonial rule. And wherever this energy headed, it was followed by the Cold War, revolutions, armed conflicts, and hot wars all over Asia.

Nevertheless, the energy of decolonization that sought independence was not endless. Once the goal was accomplished and colonial rulers were ousted, "independence as an objective" was replaced by an issue of a different nature: that of substantial nation-building. This shift paved the way for the wave of "development" that engulfed Asia from the late 1960s through the 1970s.

During the postwar era, when the world remained in the grips of the Cold War, Asia was characterized as an arena of erupting political energy that broke through the Cold War framework in the form of rampant revolutions and armed confrontations. Yet, this same Asia was to eventually become transfigured into an area of unparalleled economic dynamism through rapid economic growth that was labeled the "East Asian miracle." The author takes the view that one of the turning points for Asia was 1965. What position, then, has Japan held in this historic transformation of postwar Asia?

Japan resumed its engagement with Asia in the postwar era with a "southward advance" via the route of war reparations, and expanded the scope of its activities to Northeast Asia, namely China and South Korea. Consistently present in its engagement with Asia was Japan's strong inclination to pursue the depoliticization of Asia. Japan believed that neither revolutions in pursuit of reform through class struggle nor the Cold War attempts to contain them could make the future brighter for Asia, which had been divided by the Cold War and nationalism and was plagued by wars and destitution. Rather, it was down-to-earth nation-building efforts and the resultant economic development that would lead to a brighter future. This was the vision of the world held by Japan, which had committed its own future to economic development.

By guiding Asia onto a path that values development and economic growth, Japan hoped to "depoliticize" radical nationalists like Sukarno, who persisted in the pursuit of independence in order to completely eliminate the remnants of colonialism, and the likes of China, who persisted in purifying the ideology of revolution. The result would be the emergence of an Asia united by its all-encompassing orientation toward the economy.

In an Asia divided by revolutions and wars, there would be no room for postwar Japan to advance and engage in the region after it had stepped down from power politics. Given the restrictions and vacillations that characterized the domains of Japan's military and diplomatic affairs in the postwar period, an Asia that was united and fully focused on economic development was the absolute requirement if Japan was to actively and widely engage in the region.

When the Sukarno regime in Indonesia collapsed and China steered toward "reform and opening-up" under Deng Xiaoping, Japan—which was seeking to depoliticize Asia—lavished generous economic aid on these two countries that were pivotal to the Asian order, in an all-out effort to ensure that the tide of development and economic growth would be irreversible. This is the historical context in which Indonesia and China became the number one and number two recipients of Japan's Official Development Assistance in accumulative terms. When we recall that these two countries were once the center of radical leftist forces in Asia, connected through the Beijing–Jakarta Axis, the political meaning of Japan's aid becomes obvious. It was a concrete means through which to realize the grand design for Asia envisioned by Japan.

While Japan's generous economic aid was intended to complement the US Cold War strategy to a certain extent, greater emphasis was placed on addressing the needs of decolonization and subsequent nation-building, than on containing communism, in order to "depoliticize" the gesture.

Needless to say, the dichotomy at the time pitted revolution, the Cold War, and radical nationalism against development and economic growth. As exemplified by the silent approval given to the massacre of members and sympathizers of the Communist Party of Indonesia at the time of the fall of the Sukarno regime, such "values" as democratization and human rights tended to be neglected in order to secure the political stability that was considered indispensable for development and economic growth. Those values that were slighted and left behind during the era of development found their way into the undercurrent of society, and once the era of development lost its momentum, were to resurface as the driving force of the next generation.

The Yoshida Doctrine vs. the Fukuda Doctrine

If we were to discuss these issues from a different angle, we could question whether postwar Japan had any "diplomatic strategy" or "foreign strategy" that merited the description. Among the doctrines that were explicitly named as such, two stand out as having withstood the test of time-the Yoshida Doctrine and the Fukuda Doctrine. Considering that the Yoshida Doctrine was a declaration of Japan's own choice to step down from international power politics and concentrate on economic growth, the Fukuda Doctrine may be the only doctrine outlining Japan's strategy for international engagement that will be remembered.

In August 1977, about three years after Prime Minister Tanaka was met by anti-Japan demonstrators on his travels in Southeast Asia, Prime Minister Takeo Fukuda visited Southeast Asian countries and announced in Manila the following three principles of Japan's foreign policy toward Southeast Asia. Fukuda pledged that Japan was committed to peace and would never become a military power, Japan would build up a "heart-to-heart" relationship of mutual confidence and trust with Southeast Asian countries, and Japan would cooperate positively with ASEAN and its member countries as an equal partner while also cultivating ASEAN's relationship with countries in Indochina. In what came to be known as the "Fukuda Doctrine," Japan committed itself to contributing to the peace and prosperity of the entire region of Southeast Asia based on the three principles.

The first principle can be regarded as an outward reiteration of the Yoshida Doctrine, which acknowledged Japan's past military invasion. The second principle was Japan's admonition to itself against becoming arrogant as an economic superpower, in light of the anti-Japanese riots that took place at the time of Prime Minister Tanaka's trip to Southeast Asia. The third principle stated Japan's intent to promote reconciliation between ASEAN, which had an inherently anti-Communist inclination, and the Indochinese socialist countries, including Vietnam. This was Japan's attempt to depoliticize Southeast Asia, which was showing signs of becoming a front line of Sino-Soviet confrontation after the fall of Saigon and the end of the Vietnam War.

In other words, the third principle expresses Japan's intention to "depoliticize" Southeast Asia in the post-Vietnam War era by eliminating the Sino-Soviet confrontation from the region and subsequently shifting Southeast Asia "from a battlefield into a marketplace" (to borrow an expression introduced by Prime Minister Chatichai Choonhavan of Thailand in the late 1980s). However, any attempt at realizing the third principle was to fail as the world began to move toward the Second Cold War in the 1980s.

Nevertheless, the two widely recognized doctrines of postwar Japan that survived the ebb and flow of the times were both based on the twin pillars of economic orientation and "depoliticization," indicating that they had indeed been the main pillars supporting Japan's politics and foreign affairs in the postwar era. While postwar Japan may have effectively stepped down from the stage of international power politics, this did not mean Japan's interest in the outside world was limited to its economic advance. The "depoliticization" of Asia through development and economic growth—though distinct from that of diplomacy or power politics in the narrowly defined sense—was in fact no different from "politics" in a neighboring field.

Twenty-first-century Asia and Japan

Judging by the results, we could say that Japan had considerable success in its attempt at "depoliticizing" Asia. Obviously, this is not to say that Japan had the power to lead an Asia that was inundated with the aspiration for independence, revolution and the Cold War, as well as hot wars toward stability and economic growth.

As we have examined in this book, it was above all the inherent dynamics driving Asia's postwar history that had led to the vast transformation from "politics to the economy" and from "decolonization to development." Nevertheless, it is equally true that, when postwar Asia had reached a critical turning point, Japan's economic assistance and investments played a significant role in making the transformation irreversible.

Asia's economic growth—the East Asian miracle attained by the "flying-geese pattern of economic development" with Japan at the head of the flock—greatly transformed the regional landscape, which had once been characterized by revolutions, wars, and the surge of nationalism in pursuit of independence. Japan was the hub through which goods and capital flowed, generating the dynamic vitality that was crucial for Asia as Japan had envisioned it. The 1980s was perhaps the peak of such frenzied economic activity. This transformation was also sustained by the fact that the region had been "depoliticized" under the Japan–US–China "pseudo-alliance" against the Soviet Union.

Then came the 1990s, and even as Japan went under in its Lost Decade and suffered a decline in its centripetal force, Asia went on to make great strides in economic development and interdependence, emerging as a vast economic zone that embraces Japan. This could be described as an even more successful version of an Asia "united by its all-encompassing orientation toward the economy" that Japan pursued throughout the postwar years. The framework of "Japan and Asia," which had been a premise of various postwar schemes envisioned by Japan, is now being transformed into "Japan in Asia" by the tremendous forces of real economy.

However, even as Asia becomes increasingly unified in its economic aspects, and in spite of the various exploratory efforts that are underway, it cannot yet be said that a stable regional framework has been constructed when seen from the viewpoint of politics and security.

One of the greatest causes behind the growing integration of "economic Asia" lay in China, the pivotal country within Asia, and its determined pursuit of a strategy aimed at achieving economic growth through the introduction of foreign capital and integration with the global economy. China has chosen to set aside independence for the benefit of affluence in the economic realm. But this does not apply to the realm of politics and national security. Should China continue to accomplish further economic growth and build its national strength, along with the confidence it brings, it may wish to diminish US influence in Asia in the long run, with the added incentive of "resolving" the Taiwan issue.

At present, this discrepancy between an "economic Asia" and a "political Asia" remains below the surface. But will we be able to prevent this latent discrepancy from emerging in the future? The answer to this question could determine the future direction of the Asian order in the twenty-first century.

If Asia is visited once again by a season of politics—albeit in a different context than before—this discrepancy could develop into a rupture that tears Asia apart. Should this come to pass, the fruit of Japan's postwar efforts at "depoliticization" would be lost, making Japan the least rewarded nation in the region.

The major pillars of Japan's policy options can be summed up as follows:

1 Maintain a stable US military presence in Asia through the Japan–US alliance;
2 Seek closer economic collaboration with Asian countries to promote a further integration of the region's economies, including that of China; and
3 Within the framework formed through the policies above, pursue a steady path of cooperation and effort aimed at contributing to the long-term democratization of the region.

At present, it is undeniable that the growing economic vitality and integration of Asia are guaranteed by regional stability in the absence of any challenge to the US military presence. While a long-term effort to expand a multilateral framework should be pursued in earnest, it would be unrealistic to expect any results in the short term. And for the US military presence in Asia to continue, Japan's cooperation is critically important.

The second and third points above are issues that cannot be confined to the narrow realm of diplomacy. Promoting economic partnerships require more than Japan's "advance" into Asia as in the past; the key for Japan lies in "opening" itself up to Asia, as in opening its markets and accepting an influx of people.

Likewise, the third point of offering cooperation for the long-term democratization of the region should not be left to government policy alone, but require the involvement of non-government groups and organizations. In fact, efforts with the depth and breadth that make them "cooperation" in the true sense of the word can only be achieved through the accumulation of interest and concrete engagement in specific issues, as well as cross-border collaborations, on the part of citizens and the general public.

If governmental measures for democratization end up being merely a means for one-sided imposition, containment, and countermoves, the potential discrepancy in Asia could become aggravated and more visible. We must seek ways to maximize the overlapping areas between the general direction of democratization in its broadly defined sense, and such concepts as the "peaceful rise" advocated by China, while minimizing those aspects that do not overlap. And this is where politics is expected to pitch in with its ability to shape ideas and its creativity.

We should pursue the first objective of maintaining the US military pres-ence in Asia to prevent the economic vitality of the region from straying toward competition and eruption in the political and military realms. Mean-while, the second objective should be sought to advance economic partner-ships to promote economic prosperity and regional integration even further. By using these two objectives as the twin wheels of a cart, stability in Asia could be maintained to a significant degree. However, it is also true that this basically amounts to maintaining the status quo. If we are to envisage a better future for Asia that embraces Japan, we must be mindful of the third objective, of moving in the direction of achieving greater democracy within the region, even though it might be a long-term task. While in this book we traced the enormous transformation underwent by Asia in the half-century since World War II, in the long run, it is in this third objective-more than anything else-that Asia's potential for accomplishing an even broader trans-formation lies hidden.

Afterword

In the summer of 2007, I had a chance to visit the border area between China and North Korea. Beyond a river, which forms the border, the quiet, sleepy town of Musan, North Korea, lay in the piercing sunshine. Only occasional human voices and the barking of dogs subtly carried by capricious breezes betrayed the unmistakable presence of people's day-to-day life there. The mines and factories behind the town, once some of the busiest in Asia, stood silent, motionless, as if they were relics of the past.

During the Korean War, Chinese army troops crossed this creek en masse to back up North Korea, which was being overwhelmed by US forces; this marked the full-fledged beginning of the Asian Cold War. Sometime later, the wave of development and economic growth that had originated in the remote maritime Asia in the south began to rush northward, swallowing the Chinese continent and reaching this border separating China and North Korea in a remote corner of Northeast Asia. It is conceivable that this wave could cross the river and, eventually, swallow up North Korea, a lone bastion of revolution and isolationist independence. What will Asia look like when it does?

Will Asia be an integrated and stable region supported by the centralizing forces of economics and political wisdom? Or will it face another era of instability marked by the manifestation of its underlying discrepancy and regional ruptures? In any event, this China–North Korea border will without doubt be the place that most clearly reflects the landscape of Asia at that time.

This book attempts to trace the footsteps of postwar Japan's trials and errors in Asia, which began with Japan's reengagement in Southeast Asia. The approach taken by Japan cannot be adequately understood against the Cold War framework alone, even though it had unmistakably been the central framework of postwar international politics. I am convinced that this type of exploratory exercise holds the key that is essential to understanding and analyzing Japan and Asia in the postwar era. I am also convinced that, through this exercise, we will be able to determine the historical context of Japan's relations with Asia that will allow us to conceptualize the nature of Japan's present and future engagement that is neither introverted nor imperious, but positive and open to the world.

This book owes much to declassified confidential diplomatic documents in various countries, including Japan, the United States, the United Kingdom,

and Australia. In light of the stylistic restrictions inherent to a porta-
ble paperback, I did not present each and every source of information in
footnotes.

> For more details of information sources, readers are encouraged to look
> into the following academic materials written by this author: For Chapter
> 1: See Taizo Miyagi, *Bandon Kaigi to Nihon no Ajia fukki—Amerika to
> Ajia no hazama de* (The Bandung Conference and Japan's Return to
> Asia: Sandwiched between the United States and Asia). Tokyo: Soshisha
> Publishing, 2001. For Chapters 2 through 4: See Taizo Miyagi, *Sengo
> Ajia chitsujo no mosaku to Nihon—Umi no Ajia no sengo-shi, 1957–1966*
> (Exploration of Postwar Asian Order and Japan: Postwar History of
> Maritime Asia, 1957–1966). Tokyo: Sobunsha Publishing, 2004. For
> Chapter 5: See Taizo Miyagi, "Nitchu sekkin to Indoneshia—Nichi-go-
> Indoneshia sankakoku koso no mosaku" (China-Japan Rapprochement
> and Indonesia: Exploring a Japan-Australia-Indonesia Trilateral Coop-
> eration Scheme), in *Nikuson hochu to reisen kozo no henyo—Beichu sekkin
> no shogeki to shuhen shokoku* (Nixon's China Visit and Transformation
> of the Cold War Structure: Impact of the US-China Rapprochement
> and Neighboring Countries), written and edited by Hiroshi Masuda.
> Tokyo: Keio University Press, 2006.

When I was approached by Mr. Norifumi Yuhara of Chikumashobo with
a proposition to write an original compact paperback, I was still teaching
at Hokkaido University. Unfamiliar with the format of a compact paperback, I was so at a loss in the beginning as to what to write that I hardly
made any progress. In fact, I was not even sure that I was capable of living up to Mr. Yuhara's trust and expectations. It was the graduate students
and college students at the National Graduate Institute for Policy Studies
(GRIPS) and Rikkyo University, who helped me muddle through by putting
up with my half-baked arguments during class and in seminars held at these
institutions. I am immensely grateful to them.

When I thought I had finally managed to complete the manuscript,
Mr. Kazuho Miya (presently a professor at Kyoto Seika University), who
had long been a legendary editor at the famed monthly *Chuokoron*, pored
over the details of my manuscript and thoroughly pointed out all the biases,
distortions, and oversimplifications in my arguments. I cherish that experience as an invaluable asset. I would also like to mention Mr. Takakuni
Hayama of Shosekikobo Hayama Publishing, who, by giving me the
inspiration to write this book, deserves to be called the father of this work.
Professor Takashi Shiraishi of GRIPS first introduced me to Messrs. Miya
and Hayama and subsequently encouraged me to get on with the writing
by saying, for instance, "Sometimes it works to draw a rough sketch first."
And, of course, Mr. Yuhara continued to support me all the way through
to the end by not giving up on an author who did not dare to "take off"

and by constantly providing appropriate advice from a broader perspective. I alone am responsible for any errors and shortcomings in this book, but if it contains even a fraction of virtue, I owe it entirely to the support and cooperation rendered by the four people mentioned, as well as to many other friends around me. I would like to take this opportunity to express my deepest gratitude to them.

In any event, I find the writing of history to be a presumptuous act. Writing history means summarizing grand historical events in a few lines and arbitrarily assigning meaning to the life-time accomplishments of historical figures. Perhaps the only thing a writer can do to make up for this presumptuousness is to face all the historical events sincerely and earnestly. It is my pledge to constantly ask myself from now on whether I am being sincere and earnest as I work.

Taizo Miyagi
May 8, 2008
Roppongi, Tokyo

Bibliography

Primary Sources

Diplomatic documents of the Australian government (National Archives of Australia).
Diplomatic documents of the British government (National Archives of the United Kingdom).
Diplomatic documents of the US government (National Archives of the United States).
Diplomatic Records of the Ministry of Foreign Affairs of Japan (Diplomatic Archives of the Ministry of Foreign Affairs of Japan).
Documents released by the Ministry of Foreign Affairs of Japan (requested under the Access to Government Information Act).
Foreign Relations of the United States, Washington, D.C., US Department of State (a collection of diplomatic documents of the US government).

Other Sources

Abdulgani, Roeslan. *The Bandung Connection: The Asia-Africa Conference in Bandung in 1955*. Singapore: Gunnung Agung, 1981.
Anderson, Benedict. *Imagined Communities: Reflections on the Origin and Spread of Nationalism*. London and New York: Verso, 1983.
Asahi Shimbun. "Meeting of Indonesia's creditor nations: Summary of the joint communiqué." September 21, 1966.
Asahi Shimbun. "Mastermind testifies that 'Suharto was given prior notice' in the failed coup attempt of 1965." August 4, 1998.
Chanda, Nayan. *Brother Enemy: The War after the War*. San Diego: Harcourt, 1986.
Gao, Wenqian. *Zhou Enlai: The Last Perfect Revolutionary*. Translated by Peter Rand and Lawrence R. Sullivan. Philadelphia, New York: PublicAffairs, 2007.
Goto, Kenichi. *Kindai Nihon to Indoneshia: "Koryu" hyakunenshi* [Modern Japan and Indonesia: A Hundred-Year History of "Exchange"]. Tokyo: Hokuju Shuppan, 1989.
Hatano, Sumio. *Taiheiyo senso to Ajia gaiko* [The Pacific War and Asian Diplomacy]. Tokyo: University of Tokyo Press, 1996.
Hatano, Sumio, and Susumu Sato. *Gendai Nihon no tonan Ajia seisaku* [Japan's Contemporary Strategy on Southeast Asia]. Tokyo: Waseda University Press, 2007.
Hosoya, Chihiro, ed. *Nichibei kankei tsushi* [A Comprehensive History of Japan-US Relations]. Tokyo: University of Tokyo Press, 1995.

Ishii, Osamu. "Nichibei paatonaashippu e no dotei" [Road to the US-Japan partnership], *Nichibei kankei tsushi* [A Comprehensive History of Japan-US Relations], ed. Chihiro Hosoya. Tokyo: University of Tokyo Press, 1995, 181–227.

Ito, Masaya. *Ikeda Hayato to sono jidai* [Hayato Ikeda and His Times]. Tokyo: Asahi Shimbun, 1985.

Jones, Howard P. *Indonesia: The Possible Dream*. New York: Harcourt Brace Jovanovich, Inc., 1971.

Jones, Matthew. *Conflict and Confrontation in South East Asia, 1961–1965*. Cambridge: Cambridge University Press, 2002.

Kai, Fumuhiko. *Kokkyo wo koeta yujo: Waga gaiko hiwa* [Friendship across Borders: My Secret Stories of Diplomacy]. Tokyo: Tokyo Shimbun, 1990.

Kase, Shunichi. *Kase Shunichi kaisoroku* [Memoirs of Shunichi Kase] vol. 1. Tokyo: Yamate Shobo, 1986.

Kibata, Yoichi. *Teikoku no tasogare: Reisenka no Igirisu to Ajia* [The Twilight of Empire: The United Kingdom and Asia during the Cold War]. Tokyo: University of Tokyo Press, 1996.

Kishi, Nobusuke. *Kishi Nobusuke kaikoroku* [Memoirs of Nobusuke Kishi]. Tokyo: Kosaido Publishing, 1983.

Legge, John D. *Sukarno: A Political Biography*. London: Penguin Press, 1972.

Masuda, Ato, ed. and trans. *Sukaruno daitoryo no tokushi: Su Shibo kaisoroku* [C. M. Chow's Autobiography as Told to Ato Masuda, I]. Tokyo: Chuokoron-sha, 1981.

McMahon, Robert J. *The Limits of Empire: The United States and Southeast Asia since World War II*. New York: Columbia University Press, 1999.

McTurnan Kahin, Audrey, and George McTurnan Kahin. *Subversion as Foreign Policy: The Secret Eisenhower and Dulles Debacle in Indonesia*. New York: New Press, 1995.

McTurnan Kahin, George. *The Asian-African Conference, Bandung, Indonesia, April, 1955*. Ithaca, NY: Cornell University Press, 1956.

Mori, Kazuko, and Hiroshi Masuda, trans. *Shu Onrai–Kissinja: Kimitsu kaidanroku* [Zhou Enlai–Kissinger: Record of a Confidential Dialogue]. Tokyo: Iwanami Shoten, 2004. This is a partial translation of "The Beijing-Washington Back-Channel and Henry Kissinger's Secret Trip to China, September 1970–July 1971" and "Negotiating U.S.-Chinese Rapprochement: New American and Chinese Documentation Leading Up to Nixon's 1972 Trip," The National Security Archive, USA.

Nihon Keizai Shimbun. "Watashi no rirekisho: Suharuto (5)" [My Personal History: Suharto (5)]. January 6, 1998.

Nishihara, Masashi. *The Japanese and Sukarno's Indonesia: Tokyo-Jakarta Relations, 1951–1966*. Honolulu: The University of Hawaii, 1976.

Okada, Akira. *Mizutori gaiko hiwa* [Secret Stories of Waterfowl Diplomacy]. Tokyo: Chuokoron-sha, 1983.

Okakura, Koshiro, ed. *Bandon Kaigi to 50-nendai no Ajia* [The Bandung Conference and Asia in the 1950s]. Tokyo: Daito Bunka University, Institute for Oriental Studies, 1986.

Saito, Shizuo. *Gaiko: Watashi no taiken to kyokun* [Diplomacy: Lessons Learned from Personal Experience]. Tokyo: Simul Shuppankai, 1991.

Sato, Eisaku. *Sato Eisaku nikki* [Diaries of Eisaku Sato], vol. 2. Tokyo: Asahi Shimbun, 1998.

Shigemitsu, Mamoru. *Zoku Shigemitsu Mamoru shuki* [Memoirs of Mamoru Shigemitsu, second book]. Tokyo: Chuokoron-sha, 1988.

Shiraishi, Takashi. *Sukaruno to Suharuto* [Sukarno and Suharto]. Tokyo: Iwanami Shoten, 1997.

Shiraishi, Takashi. *Umi no teikoku: Ajia wo do kangaeruka* [The Making of a Region]. Tokyo: Chuokoron-sha, 2000.

Subritzky, John. *Confronting Sukarno: British, American, Australian and New Zealand Diplomacy in the Malaysia–Indonesian Confrontation, 1961–5*. London: Macmillan, 2000.

Suehiro, Akira. "Theory of Southeast Asian Economies," *Modern Japanese Society 3: International Comparisons (2)*, ed. Institute of Social Science. Tokyo: University of Tokyo Press, 1992.

Sukarno, Dewi. *Debi Sukaruno jiden* [Autobiography of Dewi Sukarno]. Tokyo: Bungeishunju, 1978.

Taguchi, Mitsuo. *Ajia wo kaeta kudeta: Indoneshia 9.30 jiken to Nihon taishi* [The Coup d'état That Changed Asia: The 9/30 Incident in Indonesia and the Japanese Ambassador]. Tokyo: Jiji Press, 1984.

Tsang, Steve. "Target Zhou Enlai," *China Quarterly*, no. 139 (September 1994): 766–782.

University of Tokyo Institute of Social Science, ed. *Gendai Nihon Shakai 3: Kokusai Hikaku (2)* [Contemporary Japanese Society 3: International Comparisons (2)]. Tokyo: University of Tokyo Press, 1992.

Wakatsuki, Hidekazu. *"Zen-hoi-gaiko" no jidai: Reisen henyoki no Nihon to Ajia—1971–80 nen* [The Era of "Omnidirectional Diplomacy": Japan and Asia in the Transformative Period of the Cold War—1971–80]. Tokyo: Nihon Keizai Hyouronsha, 2006.

Watanabe, Akio. *Ajia taiheiyo no kokusai kankei to Nihon* [International Relations in the Asia-Pacific and Japan]. Tokyo: University of Tokyo Press, 1992.

Yashiki. Hiroshi. "Baisho to keizai kyoryoku" [Reparations and Economic Aid], *Tsusho sangyo kenkyu 5* [International Trade and Industry Studies 5], no. 6 (June 1957): 56–63.

Index